Philippians

INTERPRETATION
A Bible Commentary for Teaching and Preaching

INTERPRETATION

A BIBLE COMMENTARY FOR TEACHING AND PREACHING

James Luther Mays, *Editor*
Patrick D. Miller, Jr., *Old Testament Editor*
Paul J. Achtemeier, *New Testament Editor*

FRED B. CRADDOCK

Philippians

A Bible Commentary
for Teaching and Preaching

John Knox Press
Louisville

Library of Congress Cataloging in Publication Data

Craddock, Fred B.
  Philippians.

  (Interpretation, a Bible commentary for teaching and preaching)
  Bibliography: p.
  1. Bible. N.T. Philippans--Commentaries.   I. Title.
II. Series.
BS2705.3.C73   1985   227'.607   84-47797
ISBN-13: 978-0-8042-3140-4
ISBN-10: 0-8042-3140-0

© Copyright John Knox Press 1985

19 18 17 16 15 14 13 12

Printed in the United States of America
John Knox Press
Louisville, Kentucky 40202-1396

SERIES PREFACE

This series of commentaries offers an interpretation of the books of the Bible. It is designed to meet the need of students, teachers, ministers, and priests for a contemporary expository commentary. These volumes will not replace the historical critical commentary or homiletical aids to preaching. The purpose of this series is rather to provide a third kind of resource, a commentary which presents the integrated result of historical and theological work with the biblical text.

An interpretation in the full sense of the term involves a text, an interpreter, and someone for whom the interpretation is made. Here, the text is what stands written in the Bible in its full identity as literature from the time of "the prophets and apostles," the literature which is read to inform, inspire, and guide the life of faith. The interpreters are scholars who seek to create an interpretation which is both faithful to the text and useful to the church. The series is written for those who teach, preach, and study the Bible in the community of faith.

The comment generally takes the form of expository essays. It is planned and written in the light of the needs and questions which arise in the use of the Bible as Holy Scripture. The insights and results of contemporary scholarly research are used for the sake of the exposition. The commentators write as exegetes and theologians. The task which they undertake is both to deal with what the texts say and to discern their meaning for faith and life. The exposition is the unified work of one interpreter.

The text on which the comment is based is the Revised Standard Version of the Bible. The general availability of this translation makes the printing of a translation unnecessary and saves the space for comment. The text is divided into sections appropriate to the particular book; comment deals with passages as a whole, rather than proceeding word by word, or verse by verse.

Writers have planned their volumes in light of the requirements set by the exposition of the book assigned to them. Biblical books differ in character, content, and arrangement. They also differ in the way they have been and are used in the liturgy, thought, and devotion of the church. The distinctiveness and use of particular books have been taken into account in decisions about the approach, emphasis, and use of space in the commentaries. The goal has been to allow writers to develop the format which provides for the best presentation of their interpretation.

The result, writers and editors hope, is a commentary which both explains and applies, an interpretation which deals with both the meaning and the significance of biblical texts. Each commentary reflects, of course, the writer's own approach and perception of the church and world. It could and should not be otherwise. Every interpretation of any kind is individual in that sense; it is one reading of the text. But all who work at the interpretation of Scripture in the church need the help and stimulation of a colleague's reading and understanding of the text. If these volumes serve and encourage interpretation in that way, their preparation and publication will realize their purpose.

The Editors

PREFACE

The church has long regarded the letter of Paul to the Philippians as devotional literature. This is by no means a misreading and misappropriation of the letter, for Philippians offers its instruction and encouragement to the reader with an unlabored immediacy. However, when the church has turned to the scholarly community for help in a more careful investigation of the text, it has found attention heavily concentrated at two points: the analysis of the Christ hymn in 2:6–11 and the question as to the unity of the letter. Both of these matters are significant, to be sure, but when preoccupation replaces occupation the results are partial and uneven.

I am, therefore, asking the reader to delay the rush to commentaries until Philippians is read (preferably aloud) for what it is: a letter. By its very nature a letter both witnesses to the distance between a writer and a reader and, with few exceptions, seeks to bridge that distance. All of us know this, but may forget it when we approach holy Scripture. The simple fact is, Paul was absent from the Philippians and he wanted to be present, but he was in prison. He hoped to see them soon and he knew his presence would be fruitful. However, he saw in his absence also a kind of fruitfulness. Between certainty and uncertainty about their reunion, Paul makes much of his presence and little; he makes little of his absence and much.

This letter gives us a window to an unusual relationship between the missionary apostle and a church which was his "partner in the gospel." Throughout this study we will be very aware of that relationship and what it meant for the advance of the gospel. In order not to hinder that awareness, I have not offered the usual introductory chapter piled high with issues of date, authorship, integrity, provenance, and purpose. These and other such questions will be treated at those points where they are prompted by the text itself. As a matter of procedure, I am simply asking that the reader prepare to read a letter, then read this letter, and when further study is desired, consult the bibliography provided.

The letter to the Philippians was not, of course, written to us; it was to another church in another place in another time. That fact I have tried to respect by not making simplistic attempts to collapse the distance between the Philippians and ourselves. However, this letter is a part of the church's Scripture and to designate a document Scripture is to say that it has a word for us now. For this reason I have tried to remain in conversation not only with the text but also with those responsible for interpreting Philippians for churches to whom the letter was not originally addressed.

I am debtor to many who have directly and indirectly contributed to my work, some of whom are deserving of acknowledgment here. Steve Sprinkle and the Sprinkle Lectureship of Atlantic Christian College, together with the faculty, students, and alumni of that institution, gave me opportunity to discuss my early reflections on Philippians. For that invitation and for their response I am grateful. My thanks also to the editors, James L. Mays and Paul J. Achtemeier, for asking me to prepare this volume and for graciously aiding my efforts. To Dean Jim Waits of Candler School of Theology who granted me a research leave I am indebted, as I am to those whose generosity set me free from all other obligations in order to put both hands upon this task: Jack and Aggie Bandy, Boone Knox, William Turner, and Benjamin Hardaway. And finally, I wish to thank my secretary Janet Gary who has negotiated the distance between my handwritten copy and the expectations of editors. She has worked carefully not only in my presence but also in my absence.

Fred B. Craddock
Emory University
Atlanta

CONTENTS

ABBREVIATIONS
used in this volume

AB   Anchor Bible

RSV   Revised Standard Version of the Holy Bible

TEV   Today's English Version of the Holy Bible

To
all those churches which have welcomed me
as a partner in the gospel

"I thank my God in all my remembrance of you"
Philippians 1:3

Introduction

Reading a Letter of Paul to a Church

The person who first taught the church to refer to the documents of the Bible as "books" probably meant well, but the designation obscures a most important fact: The "books" are a richly diverse body of literature. Of course, everyone knows this. Even the casual reader of the Bible will recognize the literary variety as represented by terms such as *history, law, gospel,* or *epistle.* However, the recognition has not noticeably affected the church's preaching or teaching from "books" of the Bible. Careful scholars have identified and characterized not only the major genres in the Bible but also literary forms and sub-forms within those genres. Such analyses are for the purpose of understanding more clearly the functions and hence the meanings of those pieces of literature in their originating communities, thereby aiding us in hearing and reading with more clarity and confidence. The sad fact is, many commentaries and Bible study guides, after an introductory discussion of the type of literature being explored, proceed with explanations of the text according to "book," chapter, and verse.

This commentary will try to keep the reader aware throughout that Philippians is an epistle, a letter. Philippians is not a gospel; if it were, it would consist of a series of events and sayings centering upon Jesus Christ, with writer and recipients not only anonymous but hardly visible at all. Philippians is not a collection of proverbs and maxims; if it were, who spoke them to whom, when, and where would not matter because proverbs are highly portable, equally true everywhere, anytime. Philippians is not an apocalypse; if it were, it would offer in dramatic sights and sounds the revealed details of the final outcome to which God is moving history.

The fact is, Philippians is a letter. It is not an oration (Hebrews) nor a manual of discipline (James) nor a polemic (I John) thinly veiled as a letter at a time when the epistolary form had caught on and was a flourishing form of Christian literature.

1

That the letter form is still popular is evidenced by the many "Letters to Jane" and "Letters to John" volumes on the market. Neither is Philippians a "Dear Abby" type letter, having all the marks of a genuine letter but focusing on a single issue and with the hope of publication. There is no indication that the writer or readers of Philippians ever thought it would be published, much less as sacred Scripture! No, Philippians is a letter in the commonly accepted sense of the term. As such it opens a window upon a relationship between the writer and the readers, a relationship which, by means of the letter, is remembered, enjoyed, nourished, and informed. A letter was the next best thing to being there, and we ought to try to make our reading of it the next best thing to having heard it read in the church at Philippi. We might be helped toward that end if we reflect briefly upon what it means to say Philippians is (a) a letter, (b) of Paul, (c) to a church.

A letter

Much of Paul's ministry was by mail and for all the anxieties which that fact created for Paul and the churches, we are the richer because of it. Letters were not an invention or improvization of Paul; they were quite common in Paul's time with many letters from the Graeco-Roman world still extant. The term "epistle" referred to brief personal notes as well as to formal essay-like correspondence. In Paul's day, epistles had come to have a rather standard form consisting of three major parts: salutation, body, and farewell, with variations within that structure occurring due to factors such as haste or leisure, crisis or concord, intimacy or distance, privacy or publicity. Most Pauline scholars are agreed that Deissmann erred in referring to Paul's letters as "dashed off" on the run (*Paul*, pp. 13–14) but neither are they to be compared to the epistle-essays of philosophers and statesmen. They lie somewhere between: personal, yes, but to be read to a Christian assembly at worship. Then, as now, letters served the general purpose of bridging a distance, usually geographical, and providing a kind of presence of the writer with the reader. This is obviously true also of Paul's letters, but as will be discussed below, the presence offered by Paul's letters was far more significant than was common to the correspondence in his culture.

Sufficient investigations have been made into the form of Paul's letters against the backdrop of available letters from the

2

Hellenistic world so as to provide a general consensus on the matter (briefly but clearly presented by William Doty, *Letters in Primitive Christianity*). As would be expected, Paul modified somewhat the common epistolary form due both to his unusual relationship with the recipients and to his expectation that the letters be read aloud to a Christian assembly. In at least one case, letters to two different congregations were to be read and then exchanged (Col. 4:16). Acknowledging at the outset all the contingencies that could and did dictate variations upon and departures from a pattern, Paul's letters take the following form:

> *Salutation,* containing the identification of the sender or senders, the addressees, and a greeting. Readers inclined to move quickly past this to get to the meat of the matter will miss a world of information plus clues as to the mood and content of the letter.
>
> *Thanksgiving,* occurring in all of Paul's letters except Galatians. Not uncommon in letters of the time but modified by Paul to shift attention from the writer to expressions of gratitude for the readers. As we will observe in the commentary to follow, Paul's thanksgivings usually give a summary of the content of the letter, provide an eschatological reference for all that has been and is being said and done, and offer indirectly and subtly a word of exhortation.
>
> *Body of the Letter,* consisting of at least three elements:
> 1) theological, ecclesial, practical matters that occasion the letter (this may be a single critical issue [Gal.], a series of problems reported to Paul [I Cor.], or a few less critical matters that do not control the mood and content of the letter [I Thess.]);
> 2) autobiographical references (Paul's uses of such references vary from recalling personal associations to offering his own life or labor as a pattern for the reader, to defending his behavior, his message, or his authority as an apostle. To see the range of functions of such autobiographical references note Gal. 1:11—2:14; I Thess. 2:1–12; I Cor. 9; II Cor. 1:8–10; 7:5; 12:1 ff.);
> 3) travel plans (Paul usually expresses regret about his

3

absence, sometimes explains the conditions hinder-
ing an earlier hoped-for visit, sometimes sends one
of his associates to help the church in the interim,
and almost always promises that he himself will
come soon.).

Moral and Ethical Instruction (often referred to as "paraenesis"), which may follow a theological discussion
upon which it is based (Rom. 12:1–21; Gal. 5:1–26) or
may be located throughout a letter in which Paul is
responding to questions that have moral and ethical
implications (I Cor.) or, as in the case of Philippians,
paraenesis may be closely tied to discussions of the
relationship between writer and readers.

Closing, which in correspondence of the Hellenistic culture consisted of a wish for good health and farewell.
For Paul, however, the closing included often an en-
largement upon the circle of greetings plus benedictions and/or a doxology.

Having noted these principal features of Pauline letters, it
bears repeating that the nature and amount of attention to any
one of them would depend upon a number of factors in each
case. One significant factor always influential was the relationship of Paul to the readers at the time of writing. In the case of
Philippians this seems to have been the single most significant
factor in both the form and content of the letter. In no other
epistle, except perhaps Philemon, does the relationship between writer and reader so control the thanksgiving, the body
of the letter, and the paraenesis.

Of Paul

That Philippians is a letter of Paul himself is undisputed. In
fact, among students of Paul there are only two continuing
debates touching Philippians as a letter. One has to do with
whether or not the phrase "with the bishops and deacons" (1:1)
is Paul's or is an addition from a later period in the church's life.
Attention to that question will be given in the commentary on
that verse. The other debate concerns the unity of the letter.
Is our present Philippians a composite of two or three notes sent
by Paul to the church at Philippi? This question has been fueled
not only by a comment of Polycarp, early second century
Bishop of Smyrna, in a letter to the Philippians ("Paul, when he

4

was absent, wrote *letters to you*" 3:2), but by abrupt breaks in the flow of the letter itself. Note the unusual shift in both mood and thought in 3:1. While this feature and possible explanations of it will be offered in the commentary at the appropriate points in the text, it might be well to remind ourselves that Paul comes to us in a body of letters written to the church, preserved by the church, transmitted by the church. Paul's letters were assembled and circulated as authoritative quite early (II Peter 3: 15–16), but that was no small task. Some of his correspondence was never recovered (I Cor. 5:9), and of that which we possess, there is evidence of efforts to reconstruct letters by inserting fragments that still bear the marks of fragments. The most notable example is II Corinthians 6:14—7:1. Second Corinthians reads more smoothly and clearly without that unit. Also, if the process of transmitting Paul's letters in and for the church involved some editorial additions, as some claim of Philippians 1:1, our judgments about such matters should rest upon textual and historical evidence and not upon sentiment or preference. The point is, whatever our conclusions in each case, the investigations are designed neither to re-enforce nor to weaken confidence in the text as Scripture. On the contrary, one healthy result would be increased appreciation for the church that received and then passed along these letters. Paul's letters are documents in and for and to the church. Private reading, private assessment, and private interpretation, with a relationship to the church regarded as optional, could never have been imagined by Paul.

Paul *had* to write. His missionary style of establishing congregations in major urban centers and moving on (according to Acts, he was never in one place longer than two years, three months) dictated some type of ministry in absentia. Paul chose to write letters, perhaps because that form was closest to the oral. Whether the letter represented a transition from oral to written transmission of the gospel (Doty, *Letters in Primitive Christianity*, p. 75) and whether Paul "resisted the written word" because of the loss of that openness and spontaneity which characterize orality (Robert Funk, *Language, Hermeneutic, and Word of God*, p. 249) are not issues that demand attention here. That Paul preferred to be present rather than absent seems most naturally and most frequently the case.

However, a letter was not as poor a substitute as sentiment

5

might lead one to suppose. Paul's letters not only sought to create a kind of personal presence with the readers, as all personal correspondence does, but his letters functioned as an official, authoritative presence, an "apostolic parousia," as though Paul himself were there. Robert Funk has made the point about Pauline epistles in persuasive fashion ("The Apostolic Parousia," *Christian History and Interpretation*, pp. 249–68). However, Funk has recognized that Philippians does not fit the pattern in that Paul does not, as elsewhere, group together the elements that comprise the epistolary apostolic presence (p. 262). And why is that? Apparently Paul did not feel the need in the case of the Philippian church to make a strong assertion of his apostolic authority and hence no need to declare his writing to be a surrogate for his own presence. In fact, it is the case in Philippians that not only does Paul's absence not have to be covered by strong assertions of apostolic authority through a letter, but even the anticipation of his seeing them again carries none of the force that his visits ordinarily did: threat (I Cor. 4:18–21); stern warning (II Cor. 13:10); gentle persuasion (Philem. 21–22); or appeal for financial support (Rom. 15:22–29). In other words, Paul writes of his presence with them, but then discounts its importance. The result is an epistle of "intimate distance" with the interplay of presence and absence providing the structure for the letter. Note: He recalls his presence among the Philippians (1:3–11); he describes his situation now that he is absent (1:12–26); he hopes to be present again soon, but present or absent they are to live the gospel (1:27—2:16); again he hopes to be present, but in his absence Timothy and Epaphroditus are being sent (2:17–30); however, present or absent they are to live the gospel (3:1—4:9); in fact, through their gifts, for which Paul is grateful, they are working together again as in the past (4:10–20). Intimate distance is no simple expression of feeling; Paul regards the relationship between himself and the church as ground for instruction and exhortation. There are in the letters two major presentations of the Christian life (1:27—2:16 and 3:1—4:9) and each is preceded immediately by Paul's soliloquy-like reflections upon approaching death and yet clear hope of a visit to Philippi. Nowhere in Paul's letters, with the exception of Philemon, is the relationship between writer and readers asked to carry so much of the freight. How were the Philippian Christians to hear it? How are we to understand it? If the case of Paul

6

and the Philippians was unique, we can study it as a historical phenomenon; if it informs ministerial leadership and congregational life, what is being said?

To a church

Paul's letters are personal but not private; he wrote to "all the saints." Even Philemon which by its title gives the impression of being to an individual is actually to Philemon and Apphia and Archippus and "the church in your house" (vv. 1–2). The congregation which received a letter from Paul very likely was a house church, the most common form of Christian assembly in the New Testament. We can safely assume that "house church" is not simply a term to designate where the Christians met but that the structure and behavior of the household as a social institution had a major influence in shaping the young churches. Most likely the congregation received the letter while assembled for worship. Paul was certainly aware that his words would be read in a worship setting and so filled his epistles with confessions, hymns, doxologies, eulogies, prayers, and benedictions. A writer at worship addressing a group at worship is a fact not to be missed by all others who read the letter, including ourselves. When the conditions of writer and reader are similar, new dimensions of understanding are opened. A letter from a soldier on a battlefront, written during a brief late-night respite from bombardment, is not best understood if read at the beach while partying with friends. More than dictionaries and commentaries are needed if midnight and high noon are to communicate. Nowhere in Paul's writing to Corinth does he better express the communicative distance between himself and that church than when he says: You are wise, we are fools; you are rich, we are poor; you are kings, we are slaves; you are strong, we are weak; you are held in honor, we are garbage (see I Cor. 4:8–13). It was not so, however, between Paul and Philippi; they have been partners in giving, receiving, working, and rejoicing. Even now, the same agony Paul knows is that which they also are experiencing. This fact more than any other accounts for what some call the beauty, others the simplicity, others the warmth, and yet others the spirituality of the letter.

Very likely all of these factors related to this particular correspondence have served to give Philippians so central a place in the reading of Scripture in Christian worship. All lectionaries use well over fifty percent of Philippians and some as much as eighty-five percent. Philippians 1:3–11 is often an Advent reading and Philippians 2:5–11 is always the Epistle for Palm Sunday.

To say a letter of Paul was read in an assembly of Christians at worship is also to be reminded that the congregation received it by the ear not the eye. This is assuming that the practice of reading aloud Paul's letters (I Thess. 5:27; Col. 4:16) was a general one. After all, there was only one copy. This being the case, we may be sure that Paul would write for the ear. This means that the contents would be framed so as to be understood and remembered from having heard it. We would expect, therefore, that Paul would follow a pattern of letter writing familiar to his readers, that he would use some materials already known to them, such as hymns, confessions, and good conduct lists, and that he would employ such rhetorical devices as would aid a listener. In the commentary to follow, we shall have occasion to notice many such features in Philippians.

Finally, to say that a letter is to a church is to become very aware of that church: its circumstances, its work, its strengths, its problems. Paul wrote letters to congregations, not to the church universal; and whatever timelessness there was to his letters was a matter for others to discern and immortalize. Paul wrote no third-class circulars addressed to "Occupant, Graeco-Roman World." His ministry was to particular groups trying to live out the gospel in concrete ways. So important to him were the crises and shifts of circumstance in the churches that Paul would send much needed aides for news or even interrupt his own mission in order to learn how it was with a troubled congregation (II Cor. 2:1–13). His effort as preacher and teacher was to effect an indigenous hearing of the gospel. He did not, of course, wait until he arrived in a city in order to discover what to preach; he brought with him the tradition. The categories, the accents, the contours of his message, however, were appropriate to the condition of his hearers. To appreciate this feature of Paul's letters one has only to look at the later epistles of the New Testament. In them both writer and reader lose addresses and identities in epistles that go out to all of like faith (II Peter), to the twelve tribes of the dispersion (James), to all Christians scattered throughout Asia (I Peter). Not so with Paul. Mixed in the chemistry of his letters one finds always some of the local soil. Any interpreter who would be true to Paul will do the same thing, when bringing one of his letters to a new address.

8

OUTLINE OF THE LETTER

SALUTATION

Paul Greets the Church and Its Leaders

PHILIPPIANS 1:1–2

According to the custom of his day, and quite unlike our own, Paul uses the threefold salutation: signature, address, and greeting. However, much like our own correspondence, the signature reveals a great deal about the mood, purpose, and content of a letter as well as the relationship between writer and reader. One can look at a signature and determine if the letter is formal or informal, official or casual, between friends or strangers. Paul's signatures are no less revealing and the reader of Paul's letters should pause to savor them. His lengthy (six verses!) signature with full credentials in the Roman letter tells the reader Paul is writing to strangers; the cold and official signature in Galatians announces tension immediately; whereas the warmly emotional signature in Philemon alerts the reader that Paul will be using the relationship as ground for asking a favor. Here in Philippians the absence of Paul's usual credentials as an apostle says that his relationship with the readers makes that unnecessary; but neither does Paul permit his affection for the Philippians to substitute for the central subject matter: the gospel. Being friends of the pastor is not to be equated with being the church. He prefers to sign his name "Paul a servant (slave) of Christ Jesus," flavoring the entire letter, for he will call upon them to be servants of one another just as Christ himself took the form of a servant (2:7). Here as elsewhere Paul adds to his name that of his associate in ministry. This does not mean that Timothy coauthored the letter— Paul writes in the first person singular (1:3)—but that Paul always worked as part of a team. In this case Timothy was not only well known to the church at Philippi, having been with Paul at its founding and having visited there more than once (Acts 16; 19:22), but he was soon to be sent to Philippi as Paul's emissary (2:19–23).

11

The letter is to "all the saints in Christ Jesus." The term "saints" or "holy ones" refers primarily to God's act of claiming them as God's people, consecrated, bound in a covenant (Exod. 19:6; Deut. 7:6). It is in a derived sense that the term came to refer to the moral character of those so set apart, but this secondary meaning should not be negated in order to underscore the primary one. Paul knew perhaps better than we how easily grace can degenerate into sentimental "acceptance" without moral earnestness.

Paul gives the saints two addresses: "in Christ Jesus" and "in Philippi." He will elaborate upon this double designation later when he calls upon them to let their life in Christ Jesus be evident in their life in Philippi (2:5). Paul will not let them forget, as though they could, that they had been called to be God's people in that time and place.

And how strategic it was for the whole Christian mission! Located on the Egnatian Way, nine miles from the port of Neapolis, Philippi witnessed daily the traffic of commerce, culture, and religion between East and West. Philip of Macedon, father of Alexander the Great, had rebuilt the town of Krenides and had given it his own name. It had flourished because of the gold mines nearby, but those days were gone. It now flourished as a Roman colony, having been favored by both Mark Antony and Octavius following their victory over the armies of Brutus and Cassius, assassins of Julius Caesar, on the plains of Philippi in 42 B.C. Antony settled some of his soldiers there and Octavius, now Caesar Augustus, located Italian families there soon after 30 B.C. Philippi is now a Roman colony, an administrative center of the Empire whose proud inhabitants are Roman citizens and whose official language is Latin. Luke provides our only account of the beginning of the Christian mission there (Acts 16: 11–40). In response to a vision and call to "Come over to Macedonia and help us," Paul and companions made a slow start at a riverside place of prayer. Lydia and some others responded but difficulties mounted. Victimized by local anti-Semitism and charged with civil disobedience, Paul and Silas endured beatings and imprisonment. As far as we know, this was the first time Paul came up against Roman power. He remembered in a letter to the Thessalonians how he had "suffered and been shamefully treated at Philippi" (I Thess. 2:2). According to Luke, Paul made at least two other visits to Philippi (Acts 20:1–6), but the political and social climate appar-

12

ently did not improve. In fact, the church at the time of this letter is "engaged in the same conflict which you saw and now hear to be mine" (1:30). Most likely the common agony helped forge the bonds holding Paul and this church together.

Singled out for special mention in addressing all the saints are "bishops and deacons" (no definite articles are used). This reference is noticeable by its singularity in Paul's letters. That fact, coupled with the common assumption that such offices were yet a generation or two from appearing in the church, has convinced many scholars to regard the phrase as an editorial addition at the time Paul's letters were gathered and granted wider authority in the church. Such certainly may have been the case, but original or editorial, the reference is not to ecclesiastical positions such as were later to be so designated. The terms, now clerical, were in that culture rather common, referring to overseers or superintendents and servants or attendants. Deacon was a common term for servant and an overseer could be a state or local official or a leader of a religious guild. As such these persons were responsible for collecting, managing, and distributing taxes or other funds. It is practically impossible to document the evolution of church order, but it is quite possible that some persons in the church at Philippi functioned in such a capacity. After all, a prominent feature of Paul's relation to this church is their gifts to him, their repeated support for his mission (4:10–20), and their generous offerings for the famine victims among the Christians of Judea (II Cor. 8—9).

Paul's greeting to the churches, "grace and peace" has become almost as familiar as his name. The double greeting was a compound derived from his heritage as a Jew and his mission as an apostle to the gentiles. "Peace" *(shalom)* reminded Paul that his gospel had been promised through the prophets in holy Scripture and that, for all his battles with legalistic distortions of Judaism, Paul was still an Israelite (Rom. 11:1). "Grace" *(charis)* was a Christianized modification of the common Hellenistic greeting *(chairein)*. Whether or not, as some have speculated, Paul began his preaching by "saying the blessing" of grace and peace from God through Christ, it is difficult to imagine that it ever became routine for him. After all, Paul's earlier zealous defense of his Jewish tradition and his violent persecution of the group that in the name of Jesus "said grace" upon all without distinction of Jew or gentile never faded from memory. It was that past which made his blessing of grace and peace a miracle

13

every time he said it. Or for that matter, every time anyone says it. Given the sinful conditions that determine our granting or withholding a blessing, for any of us to desire God's unmerited favor upon other persons is certainly due to the presence in us of a God who sends sun and rain upon good and evil alike (Matt. 5:45) and who is kind even to the ungrateful and selfish (Luke 6:35).

Paul Is Grateful for His Relationship with the Church

PHILIPPIANS 1:3–11

That 1:3–11 is a literary unit is apparent. In both content and form this passage is distinct from the verses which precede and follow it. In addition, 1:3–11 has its own identity in what is now commonly referred to as "the Pauline Thanksgiving." That the expression of thanks is confined to verses 3–6 is no reason to limit the Pauline thanksgiving in Philippians to those four verses. As was noted in the Introduction, Paul modified the thanksgiving formula common to letters of his time to include not only a statement of gratitude for the readers but autobiographical items, a summary of matters to be discussed, implicit or explicit exhortations and eschatological references. If this thanksgiving seems a bit long for a brief letter, one has only to read Paul's other letter to a Macedonian church, First Thessalonians, to discover that the thanksgiving can be more than one-half the entire epistle.

Having satisfied ourselves about the unity of 1:3–11, it remains our task to discern any internal pattern to the passage which would aid hearers (not readers) to grasp and hold in mind the contents. The thanksgiving here has a threefold structure which may be viewed in either of two ways: In content, there is the expression of gratitude (vv. 3–6), the expression of Paul's affection for them (vv. 7–8), and the expression of a prayer for the church (vv. 9–11). In terms of movement, however, the passage can be viewed in terms of Paul's relation to the Philippians' past (vv. 3–6), present (vv. 7–8), and future (vv. 9–11). Comments on the text will follow this latter perspective because it maintains the centrality of the writer-reader relationship and because it does not give the impression, as does the former

15

analysis, that thanksgiving, participation, and petition are distinctly separate categories in Paul's joyful reflection.

Philippians 1:3–6
The Past: How It Has Been Between Paul and the Philippians

To begin with a word of thanksgiving was not unusual for any correspondent of that day, but for Paul it was theologically central and essential. Having expressed the blessing of God's grace in the greeting (v. 2), the clear responding word was "thanks." Even in English one can see the word "grace" *(charis)* in the word "I give thanks" *(eucharisto)*. In fact, Paul can sometimes use exactly the same word for grace and gratitude (II Cor. 9:14–15). If the action is from God to us, the translators render it grace; if from us to God, gratitude. Paul testifies to what the heart already knows: Giving and receiving are really so much alike, one word can define both.

That for which Paul is grateful is twofold, stated in parallel phrases: his remembrance of them (v. 3) and their partnership in the gospel (v. 5). Actually, the Greek text translated "all my remembrance of you" can also be translated "all your remembrance of me." In the latter rendering, Paul would have clearly in mind their gifts to him. While that fact in their relationship is imbedded in the words partnership and partakers (vv. 5, 7) and will receive full treatment in 4:10–20, the entire orientation of 1:3–11 makes "all my remembrance of you" more appropriate here. In circumstances which could understandably breed doubt, despair, even bitterness, Paul remembers and is grateful. It was his legacy as a Jew to survive and even to flourish in painful difficulties by remembering Abraham, the exodus, the temple, the promises. Paul already knew before conversion that being a believer is to a large extent an act of memory. It still is, as some early Christians understood when they referred to being lost in the world as a "having amnesia." Secondly, Paul is thankful "for your partnership in the gospel from the first day until now" (v. 5). From the time of his arrival in Philippi, Paul experienced the faithful as participants, partners, partakers, sharers. The word *koinonia*, to have in common, is variously translated according to what is being shared: money, suffering, work, or grace. Its frequency in the letter (1:5, 7; 2:1; 3:10; 4:14) testifies to the full identification of the Philippians with Paul's message and mission. Our common translation of this rich New Testament word is "fellowship" but that overused and misused word probably will not carry the freight any more. For the church today to announce a meeting for the purpose of fellowship is in essence to promise all attending that there will be no serious business, no worship, no work. Given the degeneration of language, one has to say something different in order to mean the same thing.

In the sub-unit verses 3–6, verse 4 is parenthetical. One wonders why Paul separates the two matters for which he is grateful with a note to the effect that he always prays for all of them with joy. The impression is that the relationship between Paul and the Philippians, strong and beautiful as it was, suffered from some nagging minority report. If so, what in the parenthetical comment is to be underscored? It could be the word *all*; that is, Paul prays for all of them, not a favored few. Paul certainly uses *all* noticeably (vv. 4, 7, 7*b*, 8), and later comments reflect some tension and disunity (2:1–11; 4:2–3). Or the key word may be *joy*. It is common to refer to Philippians as the epistle of joy, but one does wonder why the word occurs so very frequently. Perhaps we are unduly suspicious of writers and speakers who say some words too often. Here it may be as simple a matter as trying to assure close friends who are heavy with the news of Paul's imprisonment that being in prison and facing death have not robbed him of joy. Or, it may be that the Philippians, themselves suffering hostility and conflict (1:28–30), have lost their joy; and Paul knows that if they can see that he remains joyful, they might recover their own.

Just as Paul began in verse 3 with thanks to God, he comes now full circle in verse 6 to look beyond the Philippians and himself to the God whose own "good work" the church is, including both Paul and the Philippians. Paul's confidence is expressed with his characteristic symmetry: The one who started the work of grace in Philippi will not abandon it in a state of incompleteness. God will complete, finish, bring to fulfillment, perfect that work "at the day of Christ Jesus." This eschatological reference to the day of Christ recurs at verse 10 and at that point will draw more detailed attention.

17

Philippians 1:7–8
The Present: How It Is Between Paul and the Philippians

In this brief passage Paul's expression of affection for the Philippians is stronger than any other in his letters, with perhaps the exception of his statement of attachment to his own people, the Israelites (Rom. 9:1–5). This is true, that is, if one translates the difficult clause in verse 7 "I hold you in my heart" (RSV) rather than "you hold me in such affection" (NEB). The Greek construction permits either, but the Revised Standard Version is much preferred here because what is being so strongly stated, if not argued, has nothing to do with whether the Philippians hold Paul in deep affection. And it hardly fits Paul's relationship with any church to say he feels the way he does because they feel the way they do. Nowhere in Paul's letters does one get the impression that his love waited for the phone to ring. We have no reason to doubt his sincerity when he says his love is the very love of Christ (v. 8) which was, of course, an initiating love, not a love reacting to the initiative of another.

The central feature of Paul's statement of affection in verses 7–8 is precisely the unusual strength of his assertion. In fact, the statement is not simply strong, it is in the language of persuasion. Notice his line of thought in verse 7: It is right, just (I am justified) to think, feel, be oriented toward you (the word translated "feel" is a favorite and important one in Philippians. It means frame of mind, attitude, life direction; cf. 2:2, 5; 3:15, 19; 4:2, 10). Why would Paul even have to assert that "it is right" or "he is justified" in feeling as he does? Then he states the grounds of his justification: because I hold you in my heart. Then even that is given justification: You are all partners with me of grace, says Paul, both in imprisonment and in the defense and confirmation of the gospel.

18

Before exploring further this unusual statement of love, framed and mounted as though there were doubters or opponents, we ought to attend to some of the remarkable phrases within it. The Philippians are "fellow sharers," a redundant expression to reflect how totally they have identified with Paul's mission. Paul, though, does not call it mission or work but grace (v. 7). While we would expect any elaboration upon grace to involve affirmations of redemption, Paul surprisingly relates grace to prison bonds and courtroom scenes. What have such modifying expressions to do with grace? Paul elsewhere refers to his ministry as grace (Rom. 1:5) and shortly will be saying to these Philippians that it has been granted (graced) to them to suffer for Christ and to engage in the same conflict which was Paul's (1:29–30). Such grace participates in the very suffering of Christ (3:10).

The present form of that grace for Paul is prison. He does not say what precipitated his arrest nor what the accusations were. He only says his imprisonment is "for Christ" (1:13). Whatever its originating causes, his imprisonment was not a matter to be handled by religious authorities settling a synagogue-church clash. References to the praetorian guard (1:13) and those of Caesar's household (4:22) tell us Paul is in the powerful hands of Roman authority. Paul is apparently being held in a barracks or guardhouse where Roman officials and supporting military are quartered. Imprisonment was for persons awaiting trial and not punishment following conviction; therefore, "jail" could be a house, a cave, a barracks, or any secured room. Mention of the praetorium means that Paul is in an imperial city, but which one is not known. Rome has been traditionally the favorite guess but Caesarea and Ephesus were also imperial cities. Most of the commentaries debate the pro's and con's of Rome, Caesarea, and Ephesus as sites of Paul's imprisonment and easy access to those arguments make a rehearsal of them here unnecessary (see Bibliography). Wherever he is and on whatever charges, Paul uses the technical language of the legal process: "imprisonment and defense and confirmation (vindication) of the gospel." Whether his use of courtroom terms is to be taken literally as trial appearances (as does the NEB, "when I lie in prison or appear in the dock to vouch for the truth of the Gospel") or only symbolically (as does the TEV, "in prison and also while I was free to defend and firmly establish the gospel"), what is clear is that while it is Paul who is in prison he understands that it is the gospel which is on trial. Any thought of distancing himself from the gospel for his own security apparently never entered his mind.

19

The one matter about which Paul does defend and justify himself is his feeling for the Philippians. As though he had not done so adequately in verse 7, he speaks even more strongly in verse 8. As though he were on trial in their eyes, Paul calls on God as witness in his behalf and characterizes his love as that of Christ himself. Paul's yearning for them is with "the affection *(viscera)* of Christ Jesus." The signals are too clear to miss: verses 7–8 and the parenthetical verse 4 reflect a problem in Paul's relationship with the church at Philippi. The exact nature of the matter is not clear, but it does seem to be an issue of intimacy, not distance. Has Paul been very close to some members while others felt slighted? Is it the nature of and not the fact of Paul's affection that needs justification? Have other churches been critical of Paul's apparent favoritism toward Philippi? After all, this same missionary who absolutely refused to take a dime from another church, even when in dire need (II Cor. 11:8–11), accepted money repeatedly from Philippi. Or is the problem all in the supersensitive mind of Paul who senses he may have lost the delicate balance between intimacy and distance appropriate to the ministry? Whatever we may conclude in the process of reading the text, the thanksgiving (1: 3–11) has alerted us that the letter will deal with at least two subjects: Paul's own personal situation and his relationship with the church at Philippi. If that is in fact the case, we can anticipate having to think through again issues of ministerial relationships, professional distance, the need to belong and yet the dangers of intimacy, and the whole question of what it is which characterizes relationships as Christian. Doctors and lawyers have clients and they have friends, but only ministers have congregations.

Philippians 1:9–11
The Future: How Paul Hopes It Will Be with the Philippians

20   In characteristic fashion, Paul concludes the thanksgiving with an eschatological reference (cf. also I Cor. 1:7; II Cor. 1:10; I Thess. 1:10). The central image of the reference is "the day of Christ" (v. 10; also 1:6; 2:16). The day of Christ is a Christianized

version of the day of the Lord in the Old Testament (Amos 5:20; Zeph. 1:14) and refers to the Parousia, the coming of Christ. The image is here unadorned with the end of time descriptions: afflictions, struggle of good and evil, cosmic turmoil, resurrection and judgment. However, the simplicity of the reference is no ground for saying Paul had by this time lost interest in the eschaton. All his discussions, theological, ecclesiological, and ethical, were bordered by an eschatological reservation. God began the work and God will bring it to conclusion.

The controlling image is the day of Christ but the form of the reference is prayer. Just as Paul opened with a twofold thanksgiving, he concludes with a twofold petition. First, he prays that the Philippians will grow and mature in love. Not a love that is sentimental and easy and grins at the wrong time; not a love that shrinks from truth-telling and tough engagements; but a love that is joined to knowing and understanding, to probing and discerning, to putting itself to the test in real-life situations and making moral choices in matters that count (cf. Rom. 12:2). Secondly, Paul prays that at the day of Christ they will be pure and blameless (having neither stumbled nor caused to stumble). There is no room here for pride or superior holiness, no reason to be keeping score, for such lives are the fulfillment of that gift of righteousness which comes from God through Jesus Christ, and such lives continually offer themselves as acts of praise.

Philippians 1:3–11 is obviously liturgical in form and content and hence appears often in the prayer and praise of the church. Because it ends on the note of eschatological hope, it also is a regular Epistle reading in the lectionary during Advent. The appropriateness for Advent is clear, for Advent anticipates the coming of Christ. Such anticipation has never in the church confined itself to the birth of Jesus, nor to the second coming, but to that presence (parousia) of Christ which is without season.

AUTOBIOGRAPHICAL DISCLOSURE

Paul's Forced Absence and What It Means for the Gospel, the Church, and Himself

PHILIPPIANS 1:12–26

That 1:12–26 forms the first major unit in the body of the letter is quite clear. "I want you to know" is a common formal opening, although in this case it may also indicate a response by Paul to an inquiry or a disturbing report as to Paul's condition in prison. The unit obviously ends at verse 26 since verse 27 shifts to different subject matter. In terms of content, there is but one subject: Paul's imprisonment and its effects on the gospel, the church, and Paul. In addition, the unit is held together by an inclusion, a literary device for providing symmetry in a presentation, thereby being more persuasive and also aiding the hearer's memory. In an inclusion, a passage begins and ends with the same key word or phrase or idea. In this case, it is the word translated "advance" in verse 12 and "progress" in verse 25. Paul reports the advance of the gospel where he is and anticipates the same will occur in the church at Philippi.

Within 1:12–26 there are two sub-units: in verses 12–18 Paul reports on the welfare of the gospel and in verses 19–26 he reports on his personal welfare and its effect upon his relationship with the Philippians. In the opening thanksgiving we had the clear prediction that Paul would make a distinction between his own personal condition and that of the gospel (v. 7). Paul is in bonds but the gospel is not, and at every opportunity he concerns himself with the defense and vindication of the gospel, not of Paul. We are not surprised, then, that when the church inquires anxiously after Paul's welfare he responds first by telling them how it is with the gospel.

23

Philippians 1:12–18
Concerning the Effect of Paul's Imprisonment on the Gospel

What the Philippians need from Paul is not simply a news report on how he is faring. That would help, of course, because just plain information can be relieving, healing, even redemptive. But for a Christian minister, a missionary, a preacher of the gospel to be arrested, imprisoned, waiting for Roman authorities to decide his fate—that is a condition which demands interpretation. One can be sure the unbelieving community had its own interpretation just as it did for the crucifixion of Jesus. If he were really the son of God, God would have rescued him. So in this case, if Christianity were really of God, if Paul were really of God, these painful and humiliating defeats would not occur. In societies primitive or advanced there is a widespread belief that there is a direct correlation between the kind of person you are and what happens to you. In fact, it is quite popular in some circles to promote faith in God as the key to health and prosperity. Very likely there were some Christians in Philippi who were beginning to wonder if their church was really of God. If preaching the gospel gets you arrested, what will happen to us? Is Paul's fate to be ours as well? What is the point of being Christian anyway? Yes, Paul needs to interpret his chains. Suffering, injustice, even death can be endured if someone can make sense of it, if it can be shown that some cause, some purpose is served; but there is no pain so sharp as an uninterpreted pain, no tragedy so heavy as one without meaning.

Paul writes his concerned friends in Philippi to assure them in joyful tones that his imprisonment has served to advance the gospel. Somehow we expected as much from Paul. After all, this is the same single-minded man who wrote to other churches, "it was *because of* (not "in spite of") a bodily ailment that I preached the gospel to you at first" (Gal. 4:13). He is certainly not whistling in the dark to cheer himself and his friends; he spells out in detail how the advance of the gospel had been achieved (the word translated "advance" was commonly used

24

to refer to removing obstacles, as before an advancing army). In the first place, the gospel has progressed among unbelieving guards and others in the Roman headquarters (vv. 12–13). To all these it has become clear that Paul's bonds are for Christ; that is, for nothing illicit is he being held but because of the gospel of Jesus Christ. This does not mean necessarily that some guards were converted. That the "why" of Paul's imprisonment was understood in itself constituted a gain. And how was it known that Paul's bonds were for Christ? By Paul's witness, supported by a spirit and behavior consistent with that witness, would be a very sound assumption.

Secondly, Paul says his imprisonment has generated new courage among the Christians in the area of his confinement and they are speaking the word of God most fearlessly (v. 14). At least this is true of "most" of them; one can hardly say of even the best of churches, "all" witnessed, all gave, all sacrificed, all took risks. We are not to assume that this fearlessness was born of the fact that the Roman military there now knew Paul was a prisoner for Christ and therefore posed less of a threat to the church. On the contrary, the confidence and courage was "in the Lord." It was Christ, or as Paul sometimes said with no difference in meaning, the Holy Spirit who gave heart to the believers so that the arrest of a leader actually strengthened the church. How different from the beginning days when the soldiers arrested Jesus; his disciples abandoned him and fled (Mark 14:50). Only by the Holy Spirit can the church experience the miraculous shift of attitude from assuming that wherever the Lord is there is no suffering to believing that wherever there is suffering there the Lord is.

And finally, Paul reports that his imprisonment has advanced the gospel in a most unexpected way: Those who preach with a spirit of rivalry and competition, envious of another's success, see in Paul's confinement a chance to get ahead and so have accelerated their activity (vv. 15–18). This is not true of all, of course; some out of love and good will increase their labors to help compensate for the loss of Paul's ministry. In that fact Paul rejoices. What is most unusual is that Paul also rejoices that the competitive preachers, operating out of partisanship (a term common in that day to describe persons hired to do electioneering), hoping both to advance themselves and afflict the confined Paul, were at least preaching the gospel.

This passage (vv. 15–18) is so unusual as to call for additional reflection. That some preach from motives of envy, rivalry, divisiveness, pretense, and with hired hand mentality is lamentable but not really surprising. We are not strangers to competition in the work of Christ, to that sense of pleasure over the failure of another's program or the decline of another congregation. In a culture which demands that we think in terms of winners and losers, even a God who desires that all win is served by persons who think heaven will be sweeter because there is a hell. In this regard, then, the passage is not unusual. What we do not expect is for Paul to say "whether in pretense or in truth, Christ is proclaimed; and in that I rejoice" (v. 18). Are we to sense in this statement a shrug of the shoulders? Is the old soldier too weary to rise anymore to reveille? Alfred Plummer comments sympathetically: "this spirit of resignation. . . . is natural enough towards the end of a very chequered imprisonment" (*A Commentary on St. Paul's Epistle to the Philippians*, p. 25). That is a most interesting interpretation, but our understanding of Paul's thought will best follow three reminders. One, these divisive preachers are not the famed Judaizers of Corinth, Galatia, and perhaps chapter 3 of Philippians. They cannot be. The Judaizers preached another gospel and for it received Paul's anathema (Gal. 1:6–9). Even a dying Paul would rise on one elbow to fight them. Here the issue is not message but motive. Two, Paul did not approve such motives; he had renounced "disgraceful, underhanded ways" (II Cor. 4:2). That he refused to permit attitudes toward himself as the canon for assessing the validity of another's ministry is not to be taken as approval of motives inappropriate to the message. Three, the power of the gospel is not contingent upon the motives or feelings of the one preaching. For all the dangers of opening the doors of ministry to charlatans, it must be affirmed that the gospel has its own life and efficacy whether or not there is visceral authentication in the preacher. Too much introspection can immobilize the church in a subjective captivity of the gospel. More is at stake than how anyone feels. Too many genuine Christian witnesses and workers have been made to feel guilty because on a given day they labored from commitment rather than a warm heart.

Philippians 1:19–26
Concerning the Effect of Paul's Imprisonment upon the Church and Himself

Some of us recoil slightly at the repetition of Paul's statement that he is rejoicing. After all, just as one does not pray and then advertise the prayer, neither does one rejoice and then say so repeatedly. Some experiences are diminished in the telling. However, two reminders are in order: In the structure of 1:12–26, "rejoice" in verse 18 is a reflection upon what has already occurred (vv. 12–18); "rejoice" in verse 19 is stated as a future, looking ahead to events not yet certain, now to be discussed in verses 19–26. In other words, Paul not only rejoices over what has happened but, because of his confident faith, also over what will happen. The second reminder is that the Philippians need to hear Paul affirm his joy, out of concern for him, but also as an assuring word for themselves as they endure a similar conflict (1:29–30).

In this passage Paul reports on the effect of his imprisonment upon the church in Philippi and upon himself. Roughly divided, verses 19–23 deal with Paul, verses 22–26 (notice the overlap at vv. 22–23), with the church. However, such division is a bit arbitrary, solely for the purpose of trying to understand a very difficult paragraph. As a matter of fact, Paul's fate and that of the church are inextricably bound together. Furthermore, as Paul will point out, both his desire and that of the church are subordinate to the will of God and the progress of the gospel. Now, admittedly, this passage is difficult to follow. It is a mixture of certainty and uncertainty, deciding but not deciding, wanting to die and wanting to live. That Paul is experiencing intense mental conflict is amply evident. He says as much: "I am hard pressed between the two" ("I am torn two ways" [NEB]; "I am caught from both sides" [TEV]). He quotes Job, the very personification of struggle, in verse 19; and the awkward grammar, the disjointed sentences, testify to the apostle's frame of mind. We have here a soliloquy, a thinking out

27

loud, in the presence and confidentiality of close friends, about dying and living. Paul is not playing at the brink of death, sensing the exhilaration of almost but not quite, and then showing snapshots to his friends. Death, the acknowledged enemy (Rom. 8:38), is near. Paul stands at the limit, curls his toes over the edge, and feels "the mist in his face, the fog in his throat." Apparently Paul needs to speak about it and the church needs to think about it. That he chose to share these resolved/unresolved thoughts and feelings with the Philippians is the highest compliment Paul ever paid a congregation. Let us stay as close as possible to his own words and the sequence of his reflections as we listen to Paul's response to a church that had expressed concern for his welfare.

In characteristic fashion, Paul begins by saying he *knows*, he is certain of, the outcome of the events which now are beyond his control: He will be delivered (Job 13:16–18). He surely means deliverance or salvation in a sense larger than release from prison; otherwise the description of his struggle is emptied of meaning. The deliverance he has in mind is not contingent upon his being released or executed. Paul's confidence is grounded in his trust in the efficacy of their prayers in his behalf and in the support of the Spirit of Jesus Christ (v. 19). The Spirit of Jesus Christ is an unusual underscoring of divine aid since either Spirit or Christ, for Paul interchangeable terms, was ordinarily sufficient (I Cor. 2:13–16). As for the present critical hour, as he awaits Rome's judgment in his case, Paul is not filled with dread. On the contrary, his mood is one of *eager expectation* ("looking out the window in anticipation" cf. Rom. 8:19) and *hope.* These words were not for Paul mere synonyms for wishing, but stood as tall and strong as "I know." What Paul firmly anticipates is that whether Rome says yes or no over his life his witness by word and conduct will honor and magnify Christ. Paul states this hope most dramatically by counterposing two vivid terms: *shame* and *boldness.* Rather than being ashamed (shrinking back, failing, Ps. 25:3, 20; 31:1, 17; 119:6) in that hour, Paul expects to be, as always, courageous, or perhaps more precisely, "out in the open" with his witness (cf. this sense of the word in John 7:4, 13; 11:54; 16:29. Shame and courage are strikingly contrasted elsewhere in I John 2:28).

28

Living or dying (Rom. 14:8), waking or sleeping (I Thess. 5:10), Paul belongs to Christ; but there is a sense in which living will differ from dying. Living is Christ (v. 21; Gal. 2:20; II Cor.

4:10, 16; 5:15), but dying would be gain. If living is Christ, what was there to gain by dying? The gain would be the avoidance of what he most feared (lest I myself be disqualified, I Cor. 9:27), the attainment of what he most desired (to know Christ fully, Phil. 3:10–14), and, as one scholar has argued rather persuasively, the release from the troubles and pain of one often imprisoned and severely abused mentally and physically (D. W. Palmer, "To Die Is Gain." *Novum Testamentum*). What if Paul does not die but is released? That, too, is an attractive alternative, for life in the flesh ("flesh" here has no negative moral implications) would give opportunity for further ministry for Christ.

Which shall I choose? I do not know (v. 22). What an extraordinary thing to say! "I am hard pressed between the two" (v. 23). Why should Paul write in such anguished terms; one would think the decision as to release or execution were his to make. Since Paul is neither judge nor jury but the one on trial, what possible meaning could there be in his struggle with his choice? Were any of us to get a letter from a friend on trial and the friend confided that deciding whether to be sentenced or to be set free was most difficult, we would begin to wonder about our friend's mental state. Has Paul suffered too much, too long? In one sense, of course, Paul has absolutely no decision; he awaits the decision of others. In another sense, though, Paul can take the initiative, walk into his own future, embrace rather than resist necessity, and be on top rather than beneath his situation. He talks as one who had done it and now is free. What can the world do to him? Even death, the last enemy, is subdued, domesticated, and could, if called upon, render Paul a most desirable service. In fact, says Paul, were I given to following my own desires, I would call upon death to take me to Christ finally and completely.

Let us pause here and make two notes to ourselves. First, it would not be appropriate to bend out of shape Paul's statement about dying and being with Christ in order to make it fit the eschatological references in all his letters. Nor have we the evidence to say Paul's views of the end have evolved from an apocalyptic vision to quiet musings about death. The whole correspondence of Paul came in too brief a time (8–10 years) to justify discussions of "evolution." He has as much right as the rest of us to discuss eschatology and to talk with friends about one's death in entirely different modes. Second, the fact that

29

this account of Paul's own pilgrimage in Christ and to Christ has been canonized as Scripture does not mean it is normative for all of us. Paul does not speak to the Philippians in the imperative; in fact, he never made his conversion, his call, his charismatic gifts, his elevation to the third heaven, nor any other such experience the rule in his churches. There is no gain in making the church feel guilty if it cannot honestly say, "My desire is to depart and be with Christ." This is not to let any of us off the hook but to realize that faithfulness in our own pilgrimages is better than talk of trips we have never taken. During the Pentecost season many churches regularly read Philippians 1:21–27, but the reading should be with respect and awe. With some texts ease and facility of comment border upon obscenity.

With verse 24 all talk of desire and decision ends because the conversation shifts to another ground: that which is more necessary. For Paul this is not new ground; his preaching of the gospel was a matter of "necessity" (a secular term referring to fate or destiny, I Cor. 9:16), not choice. Paul realizes that he is first of all an apostle, a pastor, a preacher. Martyrdom is a luxury and will have to wait.

Paul concludes this discussion, then, just as he began (v. 19), with his word of certainty: "I know" (v. 25). What he now knows is that he will be released and will return to the Philippians. This will work toward their progress in the gospel just as Paul has witnessed the progress of the gospel in the area of his imprisonment (v. 12). His return will naturally be for them an occasion of joy and exulting in Christ Jesus because of prayers answered and faith in God vindicated and renewed. Surely Paul's remark about his coming (parousia) again transposed the church's thinking into another key: Paul's parousia would be a foretaste, a solid promise, an earnest of the Parousia of Christ.

Everything now seems so clearly settled: Paul will come again to Philippi. After all, Paul said he *knew*; but the church's sighs of relief never seem to last long. They will now hear him say, "whether I come to see you or am absent" (v. 27), and again, "if I am to be poured out as a libation upon the sacrificial offering of your faith" (2:17). It is becoming increasingly clear that Paul's letter not only served to bridge distance with the most moving expressions of intimacy but also to maintain distance between himself and the church. Reasons for the latter function of the letter will appear in Paul's next remarks.

30

Whether Paul Is Present or Absent
PHILIPPIANS 1:27—2:16

It is usually helpful first of all to get a sense of an entire unit before considering its parts. It is clear even from a casual reading that 1:27 begins a new direction in Paul's thought. Whatever implicit exhortations may have been buried in remarks up to this point (and Paul is never far from an imperative), Paul now turns hortatory explicitly. Where, though, does the unit end? Most commentaries follow the paragraphing of Greek and English texts which break at 2:18. Not all do, however, and in this case the minority who conclude the paraenetic (hortatory) unit at 2:16 have made the better judgment. The reasons favoring a break at 2:16 are several. First, the exhortations proper end at verse 16. Second, an obvious symmetry is preserved by concluding at verse 16: As the preceding autobiographical section ended with a reference to Paul's coming (1:26), this passage ends with a reference to Christ's coming (2:16); and as the autobiographical section closed with Paul saying the Philippians could boast in him (1:26), here he closes with the hope that he can boast in them (2:16). Third, by concluding at 2:16, the whole unit is a kind of inclusion, ending as it began with reference to Paul's relationship to the readers and the call for conduct that is consistent whether Paul is present or absent (1:27 and 2:12–16). A final reason for ending at 2:16 is that 2:17 is autobiographical and begins a unit noticeably similar to the first autobiographical section in that it revolves around whether Paul is going to be executed (2:17) or released to visit Philippi again (2:24). The entire passage before us (1:27—2:16) is rich with images of the Christian life: soldiers, citizens, athletes, gladiators, and others, but as we shall see, it is the image of servant, of which Christ is the supreme model (2:5–11), which effectively focuses Paul's discussion of living the gospel.

31

Within 1:27—2:16 there are three sub-units: (a) Christian conduct in relation to a hostile, unbelieving community (1:27–30); (b) Christian conduct within the believing community (2:1–11); (c) Christian conduct in relation to Paul, the church's founding apostle (2:12–16). Our discussion will be framed on these sub-units.

Philippians 1:27–30
Christian Conduct in Relation to a Hostile, Unbelieving Community

Whoever read this letter to the church at Philippi was probably interrupted by applause or shouts of hallelujah at 1:26: Paul is coming to see us! But all became quiet again at 1:27: but whether I come to see you or not. The cooling effect, the sense of distance in that phrase would be difficult to miss; but what a complex person such as Paul wishes to convey by it is equally difficult to know. Had he expressed earlier that his primary desire was to come to Philippi again then his "whether or not" would be quite clear: It would be an expression of emotional self-protection. All of us have rituals which could be entitled "If I cannot have it, I did not want it." By not hoping too much one is not too badly hurt. On the face of it, Paul seems to be placing a cushion on the floor to break the fall of another disappointment. "I expect to come again to Philippi, *but* whether I do or not. . . ." Since Paul's primary desire, though, was not to come to them but to die and be with Christ, this "whether or not" cannot be a shrug of the shoulders. He is more likely being professional than personal in the sense that he must not allow those to whom he ministers to become dependent upon him. For their own health and maturity, they must stand, not lean. Paul needs no satellites whose immaturity daily confirms for him that he is a minister, and the church certainly does not need that relationship. The Christian life is not a game of hide and seek with the minister. Paul's presence or absence is not the determining factor in their living out the gospel of Jesus Christ.

Certainly not in Philippi! Proud of itself as a little Rome, official, patriotic, suspicious of any persons or movements not aligned and loyal to Caesar, probably quite anti-Semitic (Acts

32

16:20–21), this city could and did make it difficult for the disciples of Jesus. Paul knows this firsthand and so drops his usual word, which we translate conduct or lifestyle, and uses the local term for living out one's citizenship (v. 27). He means by it one's manner of life as it faces upon and intersects with life in the city. The church is not to hide nor apologize for its existence. It is possible for them, in fact, it is incumbent upon them, to live among the people and institutions of Philippi in a way that is informed and disciplined by the gospel of Christ. This is to live "worthily." "Worthily" is an adverb describing how they conduct themselves, not an adjective descriptive of their character (cf. I Cor. 11:27 in contrast to Luke 15:19). This is no easy task. It calls for standing on duty together, striving side by side as fellow athletes who are so completely a team that they function as one person, having one spirit and soul. Nothing the opponents say or do must be allowed to frighten (*stampede,* as with horses) them. They cannot assume that outside opposition in and of itself creates internal unity. Even if it did, it would be a unity defined by the opposition. Therefore, the church must struggle together "for the faith of the gospel." If they cease to act and simply react, then it is no longer the gospel but the culture which gives the church its identity. Precisely who the opponents are is not clear. They may be neighbors or officials; they may be Romans or Jews; they may operate by litigation or by harassment. We do not know.

What Paul knows, however, is that united, firm, consistent living out the gospel of Christ will be an omen, a sign, a manifestation, a preliminary demonstration of the future; and the omen will be to the opponents (v. 28). To them Christian conduct will be a sign of what will occur at the end: the destruction of the opponents and the salvation of the believers. It is important to keep in mind that the omen is to the opponents, not the Christians. Were Paul referring to a sign from God to the Christians, he would be adding fuel to an already too prevalent motivation among the saints: delight in the destruction of the wicked. The church has received from Paul instructions on how to conduct their lives; what God makes of that among the persecutors is not the church's concern. Paul is simply stating what he had said elsewhere (II Cor. 2:15–16) and what the church has always believed: The word of God is a two-edged sword. Christ effects the rise *and the fall* of many (Luke 2:34). Turning on a light creates shadows, a darkness of a different kind; that is the una-

33

voidable reality. Even the gospel, good news, *makes a difference;* and all who embrace it and witness to it have to live with that painful truth. This truth, though, is no operating principle, no motivating force. Only God deals in final conclusions.

The Philippian Christians have more than a sign, however; they have clear evidence of God's grace, for it has been granted *(graced)* to them not only to believe in Christ but to suffer for Christ (v. 29). Whether they were able to think of their suffering (the word from which we get "paschal") as a gift we do not know, but Paul has already attributed to them full partnership in his imprisonment and his trials (1:7). Human nature being what it is, the Philippians probably felt the difference between fellowship in Paul's chains and wearing their own. However, if they had drunk deep of Paul's preaching, then they also knew how special is the gift of being identified with Christ in suffering (3:10).

If such identification with Christ seemed for them too lofty an interpretation of their problems, then at least they could identify with Paul. They are engaged in the same conflict (gladiatorial contest) which they had seen when Paul was there (I Thess. 2:2) and now through this letter hear to be his present state (v. 30). To go as far as Ernst Lohmeyer, a German commentator, and interpret Philippians as a document on martyrdom may be reading beyond the evidence; but verse 30 certainly gives the impression that the Philippian church is in a situation posing the threat, if not the reality, of arrest and possibly of death. By speaking of their conflict as the same as his, Paul is not merely being descriptive, however; he is being interpretative. He is inviting the believers at Philippi, beleaguered as they are, to understand their suffering through his. That, in effect, is an invitation to understand their suffering as a Christ experience. No believer, suffering for the sake of the gospel, could ask for more.

Philippians 2:1–11
Christian Conduct Within the Believing Community

One should not be deceived by the beginning of a new chapter; the break in the flow of thought is not that major. In fact, 2:1–11 is tied inseparably to 1:27–30. The conjunction "then" or "so" (2:1) looks back to what has been said and builds upon it. The "one spirit, one soul" (1:27) quality essential for standing and struggling together in the face of hostility is now to be given increased attention as Paul characterizes a believing community that is in Christ Jesus (2:1–5). Finally, that 2:1–11 is continuous with what precedes is evident in Paul's basing the exhortation of this unit upon the two considerations which have dominated the letter thus far: the Christian experiences they have all shared and the relationship of the church to Paul.

In recalling their life as a community formed by the gospel, Paul uses in 2:1–4 a number of the key words from chapter one: joy, fellowship, love, partnership, affection, unity, and mindset or attitude (1:4, 5, 8, 13, 27); and he does so in language that assumes these experiences are already genuinely theirs. This fact is a bit concealed by the fourfold use of "if" in 2:1. In our usage, "if" most commonly expresses uncertainty or a condition contrary to fact. The Greek language also has a way of saying such things as, "If I were the king (but I am not)." That language had another way of saying "if" which stated the case exactly. For example, "If I am your friend (and I am)." This latter type of conditional clause was used to lay a foundation for a request, a command, an instruction. Such is the case in 2:1:" . . . if there is any encouragement in Christ" (and there is). One could just as well begin the four clauses in 2:1 with *"since* there is." What is important to keep in mind is that Paul is not raising any question or doubt about the quality or genuineness of the Philippians' faith and life. On the contrary, he is not only affirming them but is building his call for progress and maturity upon those very faith and life experiences. In so doing he shows himself the wise pastor. Rather than portraying their past as negative and inadequate, a dark backdrop against which to cast

35

appeals for new conversions, Paul lifts to the conscious level those qualities of common life by which the church has been identified and sustained. By rejecting the guilt trip approach Paul is able to nourish his exhortation with the most unused resource in the church: who the members are and what they already know.

The second basis for Paul's exhortation in 2:1–11, the relationship of the Philippians to himself, is not stated as an assumption but as an imperative; and this imperative governs verses 2–4: "complete (fill, make completely full) my joy" (v. 2). On the face of it, making the minister's joy complete hardly seems adequate motivation for Christian living. That appeal sounds much like the half-time speech of a coach: "Win this one for me," which is, of course, whether in locker room or sanctuary, a form of emotional blackmail. In Paul's case, however, it should be kept in mind that Paul so completely identified both with Christ (1:8) and with the church (1:7) that his joy was not his alone, and neither was it simply an emotion or feeling. The joy of Paul and of the church was, as he put it, "in Christ Jesus," nourished by their relationship with each other and by the Spirit. It must be remembered also that Paul regarded his apostleship as being authenticated not solely by his having seen the Lord but by the clear evidence that his churches were indeed churches *of Christ.* If they failed to live by faith in the grace of God and to offer themselves to each other and the world as servants after the manner of Christ, then Paul saw himself as having labored in vain (2:16; I Cor. 15:9–11). In the conduct of the church, therefore, the prayers Paul offers with joy (1:4) will be answered and his joy will overflow.

That which will make Paul's joy complete is concord and harmony in the church at Philippi. For emphasis as well as clarity he says what he has in mind in four expressions: being of the same mind (the phrase does not refer to agreeing on everything, but to having a common attitude or orientation); having the same love, being in full accord (joined souls); and of one mind (he repeats the call for a common attitude or mindset). The word twice used in 2:2 and translated "mind" is extremely important in this letter. The Revised Standard Version translates it "feel" in 1:7, "thus minded" in 3:15, "with minds set" in 3:19, and "to agree" in 4:2. By his double use of the word in 2:2, Paul is preparing his readers for his elaboration upon what the Christian mindset, attitude, or orientation

36

is, beginning in 2.5. "Have this mind among yourselves."

We do not know what lay at the root of the discord in the Philippian church. There may have been polarization around the two women who had worked faithfully with Paul in the past but are at odds with each other (4:2–3). The dissension could have been generated by the preaching of those who sought to bring elements of Judaism into the faith and practice of the church, against whom Paul lashes out in 3:1*b*–6. Or it could have been the case that the disunity in Philippi was related to Paul himself. If Paul's unusually strong insistence that he loves and prays for all of them (1:4–8) implies that some members felt they were not in the circle of Paul's favor and affection, then that could be the condition further addressed in 2:1–11. If so, that fact would also enlighten 2:2: Their unity would complete Paul's joy. In any case, we should not dismiss Paul himself as a cause for some relational problems in the church, regardless of whether or not his own conduct or words had contributed to the problem. The relationships of ministers to congregations are very complex and directly affect the relationships of the members to each other. Paul's stature as an apostle did not exempt his churches from the envy, jealousy, and pettiness that causes gossip about who does and who does not belong to the inner circle.

Whatever the cause, the problem apparently was rather serious. This conclusion is supported within the text itself. Paul not only intensified his call for unity by a fourfold description of the harmony to be achieved (2:2) but he laid a rather elaborate foundation for it in the fourfold characterization of the community's experience (2:1). Since there is encouragement (though the word may also mean comfort or help) in Christ, since there is love's incentive, since there is participation (fellowship, partnership 1:5, 7; 3:10) in the Spirit, since there is affection (bowels, the seat of emotion in their psychology, 1:8) and compassion, then, says Paul, there is adequate foundation to build a stronger community. Although some commentaries seek to distinguish between the Christ experiences and the Spirit experiences listed, most likely such distinctions did not exist in Paul's mind.

If there is in 2:1–11 any actual description of the behavior of the Philippian Christians which we have been calling discord, then it probably is to be found in verses 3–4. After being totally positive about their past experiences (v. 1) and about the

37

unity to be sought (v. 2), Paul presents the forms of conduct and relationships to be avoided. He does so by the use of three negatives: nothing from selfishness (the word was used in 1:17 to describe the "partisan for hire" mentality of some preachers), nothing from conceit (literally "empty glory"; obviously Paul is looking ahead to his portrayal of Christ as one who emptied himself of claims to glory), and not looking after one's own interests. The fact that Paul uses negatives does not prove that the Philippians were guilty of these things; that is, the expressions cannot be translated "*Stop* acting selfishly." While the language of the New Testament makes a difference between prohibitions which mean "stop" and those which mean "do not start" (there is a great difference between "stop stealing" and "do not start stealing"), that difference is not evident here because the only imperative verb, in fact the only verb, in verses 1–4 is "complete my joy." The English tries to capture the sense of what is really a long and difficult sentence by breaking it up, using additional verbs (do, count, look) that are permitted by the sense of the text. There is nothing misleading in the translation, but it is sometimes helpful to know what cannot be recovered by looking at the Greek text. It is common practice to use what a writer says as evidence for drawing a rough sketch of those addressed, but we should all be aware of the limits of this kind of circularity.

What we do know for sure, however, is that Paul regarded as inappropriate to the body of Christ the selfish eye, the pompous mind, the ear hungry for compliments and the mouth that spoke none, the heart that had little room for others, and the hand that served only the self. Paul was not opposed to individualism in the sense that one is to be responsible for oneself and bear one's own burden (Gal. 6:4–5). If minding one's own business meant an unwillingness to bear another's burden, a distancing of oneself from partnership in the gospel, an aloofness from the common joy and suffering, a coldness to all the ways we are members one of another, then such individualism is destructive of the community and a contradiction of the gospel which speaks and sings of a Christ who was first and always the servant of others. At this point Paul shifts again to the positive in order to elaborate upon that attitude, mind, orientation, way of thinking of which he has spoken repeatedly. There is, he says, a way of "minding," an approach to life, to others, to self, to God which characterizes those who are in Christ Jesus;

38

and he calls upon the Philippians to let this mind qualify all their relationships with each other (v. 5). Since the latter part of verse 5 lacks a verb, the Revised Standard Version simply inserts "which *you have* in Christ Jesus." The sentence structure would also permit as acceptable the repetition of the verb in the first clause: "Think this way among yourselves which you think also in Christ Jesus." Admittedly it is a difficult expression, and obviously Paul understood that. Therefore he proceeds to clarify in verses 6–11 what the "in Christ Jesus" mind is.

The form of Paul's elaboration is that of a hymn. This has been the generally accepted view among scholars since Ernst Lohmeyer's dissertation on this passage (1927). There is not, however, general agreement on the literary analysis of the hymn. Some, following Lohmeyer, view the hymn as structured upon the pattern of the descent and ascent of the Redeemer and therefore framed as two major strophes (vv. 6–8, 9–11), each consisting of three stanzas. Others see in the passage three strophes, each describing a phase of the Christ story: pre-existence, earthly career, glorification. Neither is there agreement as to whether Paul composed the hymn or quoted one already available to him and the church. The majority opinion is that Paul is quoting a hymn which arose in another context to address another problem, perhaps a christological question. Christological hymns and confessions are not uncommon in Paul's writings and they seem, by internal structure and relation to their literary contexts, to be quotations from a common store of materials used in the worship of gentile Christian churches (I Cor. 8:6; II Cor. 8:9; Col. 1:15–20, and others). If Paul is quoting here rather than composing, most likely he himself added "even death on a cross" (v. 8). The phrase is awkward literarily in its present location but so central in Pauline thought that the apostle chose theology over poetry.

There are other unsettled questions about 2:6–11, questions having to do with details of literary form, the Christology being espoused, the sources of the hymn, and the theological background, whether Jewish or Hellenistic or both. For those wishing to pursue any of these matters beyond the limits of this volume, a special section in the Bibliography is devoted to helpful books and articles on this passage. The hymn is so rich in statement and inference, in proclamation and implication, that the student can easily forget what Paul sought to say to the Philippians by means of the quotation. Accepting Paul's pur-

39

pose in 2:1–11 as a proper restraint upon interpretation, we will confine ourselves to the pursuit of two questions: What does the hymn say? (and more importantly here) What does Paul say by quoting the hymn?

Philippians 2:6–11 is a rehearsal of the Christ story in three movements: pre-existence, existence, post-existence. To say that Christ pre-existed, was with God prior to life on earth, is not uncommon in the New Testament (John 1:1–2; Heb. 1:1–4; Col. 1:15; II Cor. 8:9); but the passages are difficult for us because the category of pre-existence is for many of us a foreign and curious notion. It had minimal value for Judaism because the basic affimation "In the beginning, God" tended to render useless, speculations about the origins of things. Other religions of the East and Near East, however, seeking to understand the sense of human alienation in a painful and hostile world, forged out of their anxieties ideas and images of life's whence and whither. The specific meanings given to pre-existence were determined by the definitions of the central human problem. If the physical body, frail and mortal, was the problem, then some religions proclaimed the human spirit eternal, existing prior to birth and surviving death. If the world itself was the problem, then pre-existence described the positive state of life before the tragic beginning, accidental or malicious, of the cosmos. Early Christians, embracing the doctrine of creation, rejected these ideas that were sponsored by a negative view of the world, the human body, even life itself. In some quarters, however, the category of pre-existence was retained as a way of affirming the transcendence of Christ. Because in Jesus of Nazareth they experienced God, the Christians used pre-existence as one way of saying that in the very human, crucified Nazarene they had encountered reality beyond all contingencies of time, place, and history. The church has always proclaimed this paradox about Jesus Christ, but always with difficulty. Appropriate words and images are scarce. It is easier to reject the language of the ancients than to risk new categories for affirming faith. The fear of reduced or lost meaning in such linguistic transactions is understandable; and as a result, the vocabulary of the church always contains what many regard as archaisms.

40 The hymn says though, Christ did not hold on to his pre-existent state. Though in the form of God (the words translated form and likeness in vv. 6–8 are imprecise in meaning and much debated), equality with God was not regarded as some-

thing to be grasped. The expression "to be grasped" does not in itself tell us if equality with God was already possessed or was a quality to be seized, as in the case of Adam (Gen. 3:5) or Lucifer (Isa. 14:13–14). The point is, all such claims are abandoned in the choice of the Christ to empty himself. The word "empty" may be translated "in vain" (2:16) or "nothing," and is virtually synonymous with "poor" in II Corinthians 8:9: Christ was rich but became poor. The description is of Christ coming under all the conditions of the human lot, becoming a servant, obedient even to death. While Christ's obedience is, in the final analysis, unto God, very likely the statement refers more immediately to all the forces and powers that determine human life. The reader of the New Testament encounters these forces, variously termed *principalities, powers, angels, thrones, dominions, elemental spirits.* In the cosmology of Paul's time, these spirit forces were regarded as the rulers over human affairs, determining issues of life and death. For this reason, a Christ who was fully human would come under the influence of these hostile powers (Gal. 4:3–4; I Cor. 2:8), even to his death. Also for this reason, a Christ who could fully redeem would have to triumph over these powers, setting free those who all their lives had been in subjection (Rom. 8:35–39; I Cor. 15:24–28; Eph. 1:20–22; Col. 1:15–20; I Peter 3:18–22). Those who teach and preach that the saving work of Christ is solely a private and subjective experience in the heart are guilty of unacceptable reductionism. The conclusion of this hymn will make that abundantly clear.

At verse 9 the subject of the hymn changes. Up to this point it is Christ who decides and who acts, relinquishing claims, emptying himself, becoming human, serving, obeying, dying. Now it is God who acts in the exaltation of Christ. The act of exaltation includes what some writers such as Luke separate into resurrection and ascension. The Old Testament citation most frequently used in the New Testament to declare the enthronement of Jesus Christ is Psalm 110:1:

> The Lord says to my lord:
> "Sit at my right hand,
> till I make your enemies your footstool."

The name bestowed upon Jesus is *Lord,* acknowledged in what may be the earliest form of the confession of faith among gentile Christians: Jesus is Lord (Rom. 10:9; Acts. 2:36). Submission to

41

the lordship of Christ, however, is not confined to the human realm; Christ is Lord over every power in the created order. In the commonly held view of a three-tiered universe, this meant knees bending before Christ in the heavens, on earth, and in the subterranean regions. There is no place in the universe, no created being, beyond the reach of the redeeming act of the servant Christ. God's act is the vindication of what the hymn has declared: The central event in the drama of salvation is an act of humble service.

If that is what the hymn says, what is Paul saying by quoting it? We know from the context that the church in Philippi is not locked in a christological debate. We know from the hymn itself that it contains no moral messages. As for clues from any Pauline comments on the hymn, there are none, since his only insertion is to specify the manner of Jesus' death (v. 8). Clearly then, the passage is to be taken as a whole, not fragmented into lessons to be learned, examples to be followed. Whoever engages in that practice not only makes of it what Paul does not but can get caught by the exercise in an ethical snag. Moralizing on the hymn can lead to a formula for self-aggrandizement: Humble yourself now and eventually you will be number one. Contrary to the entire discussion, such thinking turns the text into a strategy for advancement and the gospel of Jesus Christ offers success and room at the top. Last now, first later! That is brief enough to fit on the lapel button of a smiling usher. A careful reading of the hymn, however, makes it clear that Christ emptied self, served, and died—without promise of reward. The extraordinary fact of Christ's act was that at the cross the future was apparently closed. As Karl Barth has expressed it, the door was locked; his obedient service came at the bitter end (*The Epistle to the Philippians*, pp. 59–60). The grave of Christ was a cave, not a tunnel. Christ acted in our behalf without view of gain. That is precisely what God has exalted and vindicated: self-denying service for others to the point of death with no claim of return, no eye upon a reward.

Whatever, then, lay in the background of the hymn, Genesis or a Hellenistic redeemer myth, in the foreground lies a church distracting itself from its witness by discord and individualism, apparently marked by self-serving behavior. In Paul's judgment what the church needs is not a scolding but a reminder of the event that created and defined their life together. In your relationships with each other, think this way, let

42

this be the governing attitude of the group, for, says Paul, that which makes the church the church is the "in Christ Jesus" mind.

It may be objected that such a conclusion as to the function of the quotation fails to make full use of this christological hymn; that is, Paul's answer would seem immeasurably larger than the problem which evoked it. After all, one does not roll out a cannon to shoot a rabbit. But such objection fails both to recognize a practice common in Paul's letters and to understand the significance of that practice. Paul understood all issues in the church to be theological, however practical they may have appeared, and so he addressed all issues theologically. In an appeal to Corinth for a more generous offering for the poor, Paul quotes one of the most beautiful and imaginative christological formulas in the New Testament (II Cor. 8:9). In trying to settle a squabble over the menu in the same church, Paul refuses to play "my motto is better than your motto" and instead recites a creed proclaiming the one creator and sustainer God and the one redeemer Lord Jesus Christ (I Cor. 8:6). All that theology just to speak to the menu? Yes. Paul did not reserve theology for seminaries and clergy gatherings; it was the church's theology, the church's faith. Paul also did not subscribe to the notion that congregational problems and disputes should be answered practically and expediently as though big questions get big answers and small questions get small answers. On the contrary, small issues could be an indication that the church was suffering from the biggest problem of all: pettiness. Paul's response to pettiness was a big answer: a hymn, a creed, a confession of faith. At stake is not so much the question of truth as that of size when the church forgets the central event which begets, nourishes, and matures the community of faith.

Those who decided that every year on Palm Sunday at the celebration of the Lordship of Christ the church should read and hear Philippians 2:5–11 acted with a wisdom beyond their own. The hymn stands in the church's Scripture not only to define lordship and discipleship, but also as a judgment upon the kind of triumphalism that abandons the path of service and obedience.

Philippians 2:12–16
Christian Conduct in Relation to Paul, the Church's Founding Apostle

This brief section both concludes the practical implications of 2:5–11 and rounds out the entire hortatory passage that began at 1:27. The Christ hymn will have its completion in the obedience of the congregation as the Philippians work out, fulfill, actualize their salvation (v. 12). The Christian life is not only a "mind"; it is diligent effort also. To this fact and to verse 13 we will return shortly.

We need first of all to get perspective on 2:12–16 by seeing that Paul concludes his exhortation as he began it, by reference to his presence and absence. In 1:27 he opened by urging a kind of behavior "whether I come or am absent." Now he concludes by calling for obedience "not only as in my presence but much more in my absence." There is no question but that Paul's presence *personally* made a difference in the life of the church. There is no question but that Paul's presence *apostolically* made a difference in the life of the church. Paul knows that, but he also knows that he must not tie their conduct directly to his presence. Otherwise the Philippian congregation is a cult, not a church. Paul wishes to set them, in his absence, in God's presence with fear and trembling. Therefore, his statement in 2:12 is stronger than in 1:27: The "whether or not" of 1:27 becomes "more in my absence than in my presence" in 2:12. Paul's mind is now tilted toward not seeing them again. This is evident not only in the fact that verses 14–16 are a farewell speech patterned after that of Moses (Deut. 31:24—32:5), but in verse 17 he will speak again of his death.

The plain fact is, Paul cannot turn them loose and leave them to God. Nothing is more vital for understanding Philippians than sensing the inseparable bond between Paul and the church, dramatically expressed in the presence/absence motif. It is not simply the case that Paul's presence or promise of coming is a motivating factor in the life of the church; his absence is equally as strong or even stronger as a basis for urging high standards in conduct and relationships. Notice that Paul

44

expects even greater fidelity and obedience in his absence. How
so? Because his absence here implies his departure in death.
What could be more powerful in the life of the congregation
than the apostle's last words, his farewell letter to them. It is
important, again, to remind ourselves that we do not have here
simply an emotional appeal, although that is hardly to be
missed. Neither are we reading lines that support a popular case
against Paul as a conceited claimant to apostleship forever
scrambling for credentials and a secure place in the affections
of the church. Rather, this letter reflects a relationship that is
substantive and fruitful in so many ways. Notice: Paul and the
Philippians are partners in ministry; they are partners in imprisonment and trial; by identifying with Paul's suffering the
church can understand not only its own but Christ's; through
Paul's coming they will experience a foretaste of the coming of
Christ; Paul's life affects them significantly, providing an occasion to exult; their life affects Paul as well, providing his boast
on the judgment day. In fact, failure in character and service on
their part would mean for Paul that he had raced but without
a prize, had labored but for nothing (2:16; I Cor. 9:24–27).
Christ, Paul, and the Philippians were in a real sense fulfilled in
each other. We can understand, then, that if some in Philippi
felt they were not within Paul's love (1:4–8), the loss was not just
personal but ecclesiological, ethical, and soteriological. We can
understand, also, that if their relationship were predicated entirely upon his presence or entirely upon his absence rather
than upon a partnership, a fellowship, a participation that sur-
vived both intimacy and distance, then it is not just friendship
that is lost but their life together "in Christ Jesus." That would
be the truth revealed on the day of Christ: Paul's chains, his
defense of the gospel, his death would have been "in vain." If
this view of ministry is too heavy for some of us, we must keep
in mind that Paul was not a professional minister; he was a
vocational minister. Called by God's grace, he said; set apart
from his mother's womb, he said (Gal. 1:15); necessity is laid
upon me, he said (I Cor. 9:16).

The sober reflections upon his work by the apostle should
not, however, be allowed to obscure the very positive attitude
Paul had toward his readers. This is clear not only in 2:1–11 but in
2:12 when he commends them: "as you have always obeyed."
Further evidence lies in verses 14–16. While it is quite obvious
that Paul used for a model here the farewell speech of Moses
(Deut. 31:24—32:3), he has not adopted the negativity of that

45

speech. Moses: ". . . I know that after my death you will act corruptly, . . ." (Deut. 31:29); Paul: ". . . as you have always obeyed, . . . much more in my absence, . . ." (2:12). Moses: ". . . they (Israel) are no longer his (God's) children because of their blemish; they are a perverse and crooked generation" (Deut. 32:5); Paul: ". . . that you may be blameless and innocent, children of God without blemish in the midst of a crooked and perverse generation, . . ." (2:15). We are, therefore, not to impute to the Philippians the grumbling and complaining that characterized Israel (Exod. 15:24; 16:2) but to understand this as an expression of warning. The people of God are never immune to this attitude, especially those enduring prolonged opposition. The perverse generation is there, to be sure, intimidating and threatening (1:27–28), or perhaps inviting and seducing (I Cor. 10:1–10); but the people of God are not merely to survive, they are to take the initiative, shining as lights in the world (2:15). Beyond the tendency to become defensive, beyond the tendency to react to the world, the church is to respond in the manner of Christ who was a servant in behalf of the world.

A final word about verses 12–16: this passage is loaded with words for "work." The Philippians are to work out their salvation; God is at work, both to will and to work; and Paul labors and by his labors will be measured in the day of Christ. If anyone fears here some erosion of the doctrine of grace, seeking alternate definitions of the Greek words will not help. The three different words used are all properly translated "work": perspiration, callouses, sore back, and bone weariness. From work, no doctrine of grace protects us; and there is no reason to protect Paul from himself in these sentences. He says nothing he has not said elsewhere. For example, ". . . I worked harder than any of them, though it was not I, but the grace of God which is with me" (I Cor. 15:10). The church is to actualize in concrete ways, in energy-burning, time-consuming endeavors, the mind of Christ. Is there not the danger of work slipping over the line into work righteousness? That danger has apparently driven some members and clergy straight to the hammock as the only place where a doctrine of grace can be kept safe. The danger, however, is not a real one at all for those who have attended carefully to Paul's admonition. Two expressions, if taken to heart, keep all Christian work within the bosom of grace: "for God is at work in you, both to will and to work for his good pleasure" (v. 13), and "with fear and trembling" (v. 12).

46

AUTOBIOGRAPHICAL DISCLOSURE

Travel Plans for Paul and His Associates

PHILIPPIANS 2:17—3:1a

At 2:17 Paul returns to a discussion of his own situation, making this unit parallel to 1:12–26. The exhortations and imperatives of 1:27—2:16 are concluded and the autobiographical disclosure begins. In content this passage has as its center neither theological nor ethical matters but brief reports on three persons: Paul, Timothy, and Epaphroditus. In a literary sense 2:17—3:1 is almost totally descriptive, rich in imagery and with repeated liturgical references. It is not clear, however, precisely at what point this unit ends. Again, the chapter division is more misleading than helpful. "Finally, my brethren, rejoice in the Lord" (3:1a) is clearly a concluding expression, especially if one uses the equally acceptable translation "farewell" (NEB) instead of "rejoice" (RSV). Most certainly 3:1b launches a new mood and a new subject. The question among students of Philippians is not whether 3:1a concludes the unit before us; it does do that. The question is whether 3:1a concludes one letter and 3:1b begins all or part of another letter. Perhaps this is the point at which brief attention needs to be given to this problem.

For a long time readers of Philippians have been struck by the two phenomena mentioned above: the conclusion-like nature of 2:17—3:1a and the radically different material beginning at 3:1b. Scholars did not invent the problem; the fact that there is a rough seam in the fabric of the letter is clear to all. What scholars have done is to make attempts at explaining it. There is no commonly accepted theory. Some account for the break by an interruption in Paul's writing at 3:1. He begins to conclude, remembers or is informed of a problem with Judaizers in Philippi, addresses it, and then resumes his farewell at 4:8. Others theorize that upon the occasion of collecting Paul's letters, all the notes and letters from Paul found at Philippi were

47

put together as his Philippian correspondence. In this view 3:1*b* (or 3:2)—4:1 is a major fragment of another letter, just as 4:10–20 is considered by some to have been originally a separate note of thanks for the gifts sent to Paul. Both views leave a number of questions unanswered; and so the issue lies unresolved, arousing the interest and curiosity of all serious students of the letter. All should remain open to fresh readings of the evidence since neither position represents an effort to discredit Paul or Philippians or the New Testament. We are dealing in honest inquiry, not subversion of faith. For a clear discussion of the matter, the introductory sections of commentaries (see Bibliography) will be helpful. A good commentary which is structured upon the view that our Philippians is actually three letters (or fragments) with postscripts is that of F. W. Beare *(The Epistle to the Philippians)*. As is obvious by now, the present volume is based upon the text of Philippians as we have received it, whatever may have been the literary stages through which it had passed.

Just as the section before us has prompted literary questions about Philippians, it also raises the question of the location of Paul's imprisonment. The sending of Timothy and Epaphroditus (2:19–30) implies a number of trips between Paul and Philippi. The church has received word that Paul is in prison; Epaphroditus has come from Philippi to Paul; from Paul to Philippi has come the message that Epaphroditus is seriously ill; from Philippi to Paul has come the church's anxiety about Epaphroditus. Now, Epaphroditus is being returned; Timothy is coming soon; Timothy is to return to Paul with news of the church; and finally, Paul hopes to come soon. The question is a natural one: How far from Philippi is the place of Paul's imprisonment? Rome is not ruled out by the consideration of distance, but the number of trips involved does argue strongly for Ephesus or some other city within the general area. The distance between Paul and the church is great enough to account for mutual anxiety, but not so great as to render impossible the number of trips involved.

The situation reflected in 2:17—3:1*a* is not difficult to reconstruct. Paul, in prison, facing trial and possibly execution, cannot come to resume his ministry in Philippi. As was often his practice, between the sending of a letter and his own arrival, Paul plans to send a trusted associate as his emissary; in this case Timothy. However, if Timothy went immediately he could not

48

give a report about Paul's fate before the Roman tribunal. As soon as the gavel falls in declaration of freedom or death, Timothy will come and after a stay of uncertain length return to Paul (provided, of course, he is still alive) with news of the church. In the meantime, Epaphroditus is being sent immediately to Philippi. He was sent by the church to minister to Paul, became gravely ill, has recovered, and by his return will relieve not only his own anxieties but Paul's and the church's as well.

A word now about Paul, Timothy, and Epaphroditus. Paul, of course, is in charge and from prison he carries out the duties of his calling. As in 1:12–26, he regards it his first duty to interpret for the church what is taking place. After all, Paul is not a news reporter; he is a theologian and a minister of the gospel. The major event to be interpreted is his own situation in the hands of Roman power. Again, as in 1:19–26, he sends a double message: I may even now be at the point of death; I trust in the Lord that I will come soon (vv. 17, 24). We have been through this before. Some commentators call it vacillation, but that hardly seems an adequate description. Neither is it the case that Paul is playing tunes on the heartstrings of the church. He does not try to cash in on the emotion generated either by his never seeing them again or by his seeing them soon. No threats and promises are in the air. What we do have, as stated in discussing 1:19–26, is testimony to an unusual relationship. Paul can share with them honestly, without careful attention to consistency and logic. Yes, he hopes to die and be with Christ; yes, he hopes to come to them soon; yes, this is very likely his farewell to them; yes, he trusts in the Lord to be with them shortly. By so talking, Paul compliments their maturity and their knowledge and love of him. He and they have been partners in the gospel from the beginning (1:5), are now partners in prison and trials (1:7), will again share in fruitful labor if he is released (1:22–26), but, if not, his death will intimately involve them as well (2:17).

Paul wants them to see his death as an act of worship. The language is not unusual for him: the Christian life is an act of worship (Rom. 12:1); the mission to the nations is an act of worship (Rom. 15:16). After all, in the final analysis, it is not with Rome we have to deal but with God. The imagery in 2:17 is strangely beautiful. The Philippians are portrayed as priests at an altar offering up the sacrificial gift of their faith. Paul's life blood is being poured out as a libation (a practice in pagan cults and in Israelite worship), the completion or crowning touch to

49

their offering of faith. Paul's executioners are not mentioned. Whatever his death meant to Rome is of no consequence here; Paul and the church are before God in worship. As in life so in Paul's death they are intimately involved. Paul wants them not only to understand this but to join him in celebrating it. No one can doubt that at the reading of these lines tears were shed in the worship service at Philippi; but if that church was as Paul described it, when the news did come of Paul's death they gathered again—for worship. "I am glad and rejoice with you all. Likewise you also should be glad and rejoice with me" (2:17, 18).

Paul's second act of ministry was providing leadership in his absence. Paul's choice of an emissary in this case was Timothy, experienced in such work (I Cor. 4:17–19; 16:10–11), known to the Philippians (1:1; 2:22; cf. Acts 16:1–5; 20:1–6), like Paul, a servant of Christ and caring to the point of anxiety about the welfare of the churches (2:20–22). As a son to a father so was Timothy to Paul. In Paul's opinion Timothy was one of a kind and so it was not a difficult choice for Paul. In fact, one gets the impression that Paul really had no choice since his other associates in ministry "look after their own interests, not those of Jesus Christ" (2:21). Who or how many "all the others" are remains unknown. Other New Testament writers speak of defections from Paul's entourage (Acts 13:13; 15:36–40; II Tim. 4:9–16). This could be expected, given the extremely difficult and at times dangerous conditions under which Paul ministered. Whether a man who expected so much of himself also expected equal commitment from others can only be surmised. Whether Paul's broadside remark about all the others working only with self interests came after having asked them to go to Philippi or was a general expression of disappointment in ministers as a lot cannot be known. Given the hardships of travel and the possible dangers both in Philippi and in the city of Paul's imprisonment, ambitious ministers would hardly see the assignment as a promotion. In fact, the satellite types among them probably saw in Paul's approaching execution a cue to attach themselves to someone with a future.

Whatever may have been Paul's demands upon his associates, there certainly is no evidence that he regarded Timothy any less a minister than himself. Timothy's signature is on the letter (1:1) and Paul's reference to him as a son is a term of affection, not subordination. Paul does not ask the church to tolerate Timothy until a real minister can come. Timothy is not an underling assigned to wiener roasts, campouts, and the benediction at the early service. It is a mark of Paul's greatness that Timothy can be a partner in ministry; those of lesser stuff would be more careful to watch the ratings. If Paul is executed, the work falls upon Timothy, a prospect that seems not to worry the apostle at all.

More attention is given to Epaphroditus than to Timothy because of the circumstances. Epaphroditus, known only here in the New Testament, was probably a convert from paganism, judging from the fact that he was named for the goddess Aphrodite. He was from the church at Philippi, sent to Paul with gifts (4:18), and commissioned to remain indefinitely with Paul to serve him in all the ways they themselves could not through mail and money. In the course of "completing their service to Paul" (2:30), Epaphroditus became deathly ill. Through God's grace and Paul's prayers he has now recovered. Paul wants to return him now to Philippi, an act which will relieve Paul (he is in no position to wait upon the sick), the church (which has heard of Epaphroditus' illness), and Epaphroditus himself (who has been distressed that the church was distressed). No doubt much of the emotional burden of the disturbing turn of events was not only concern for the health of the messenger but also frustration over what seemed a failed mission. Paul wants to relieve all such anxieties and to pave the way for a joyful return just in case there would be whispering in the church: "We sent him to help and he became a burden"; "I knew we should have sent someone else"; "I wonder if he really was sick or just homesick or scared." To dispel any such nonsense, Paul gives Epaphroditus an extraordinary commendation. In relation to Paul he is brother, fellow worker, and fellow soldier; in relation to the church, he is their messenger (*apostolos,* used here as in II Cor. 8:23) and minister (in vv. 25 and 30 ministry or service is imaged as an act of worship, as liturgy). As to his performance while with Paul, Epaphroditus almost died (from danger? from overwork?) for the work of Christ. In a hostile environment he did not retreat but risked his life to minister to Paul (2:30). Therefore, says Paul, let no cloud of doubt or disappointment spoil his home-coming. Welcome him with the joy and honor appropriate to his selfless and sacrificial ministry. When Paul said Epaphroditus completed their service to him (v. 30), he was saying literally that he "filled what was lacking in their service." Most likely Paul intended no sarcasm or implied criticism, but the expression may have motivated them to hang a bit higher the "Welcome Home" banners.

51

Whether Paul Is Present or Absent

PHILIPPIANS 3:1*b*—4:9

The simplest and perhaps most persuasive argument for 3:1*b*—4:9 as a distinct unit of material is that 3:1*a* definitely concludes what precedes and 4:10 is a beginning for what follows. But supporting evidence from within this section is somewhat less persuasive. In fact, it must be admitted that not all scholars begin at 3:1*b*; a few put 3:1*b* with the preceding discussion. They argue that when Paul says "To write the same things to you" he simply means that he realizes his call to rejoice (appearing often in chaps. 1—2) is repetitious, but they need it and he does not mind repeating himself. Much more likely, however, he is saying "In what follows (3:2–11), I know I am repeating myself but I do not find it irritating and you certainly can be safeguarded by it." Most students of the passage find concern for the Philippians' "safety" less congenial to the preceding invitations to rejoice than to the stern warnings of danger that follow.

So, 3:1*b* is a beginning and 4:8–9, after the manner of 3:1, is a conclusion; but are these brackets set too far apart, inclusive of materials too widely divergent? That the discussions are diverse is apparent: Beware of Judaizers, avoid libertines, settle internal disputes, rejoice and be at peace, and practice the virtues you learned and saw in me. Even so, the passage has integrity in that it is entirely practical and instructive and it is the nature of paraenetic (hortatory) sections to be wide ranging in subject matter (Rom. 12; Gal. 5:13—6:10; Eph. 4:25–32). However, is 3:4–14 not autobiographical rather than hortatory? No, 3:4–14 is no more autobiographical in its function than 2:6–11 was christological in its function. In fact, Paul functions paraenetically in this section just as Christ the servant did in the previous unit of exhortations (1:27—2:16). The parallels are un-

53

mistakable: As the "mind in Christ Jesus" governed instructions as to conduct and relationships, so here Paul is the one to be imitated (3:17); what they have learned, received, heard, and seen in Paul they are to do (4:9). Why so? Because even as Christ gave up all claims so has Paul, relinquishing everything so that he might be identified with Christ totally: in suffering, in death, in resurrection.

As stated earlier, the question as to whether 3:1b begins a separate letter (Beare) or is an afterthought (Barth) is here being left open. Were a firm decision in the matter crucial to the interpretation of the passage, such openness would be inexcusable; but it is not. Of course, we would like to know if 3:1a ended a letter or was another example of Paul's way of having mini-benedictions prior to the final benediction (Rom. 11:36; 15:6, 13, 33; 16:25–27). Of course, we would like to know whether Paul's repeating himself (3:1b) is a reference to a letter now lost or to teaching delivered orally when he was with them. The idea of "lost letters" nags and tugs and frustrates. Paul is certainly not repeating anything said elsewhere in this letter. This section strikes like a storm upon the serene landscape of the remainder of the letter. All we can say is that the Philippians had access to discussions unavailable to us; therefore, repetition to them is entirely new to us. After all, though, the letter is to them, not to us.

We will discuss this section in the sub-units into which the passage seems most naturally to fall: (a) look to Paul rather than to the Judaizers (3:1b–16); (b) look to Paul rather than to the libertines (3:17—4:1); (c) let Paul's associates and fellow workers be reconciled (4:2–3); (d) once more, rejoice (4:4–7); (e) practice the virtues Paul himself has embraced (4:8–9).

Philippians 3:1b–16
Look to Paul Rather Than to the Judaizers

The threefold "Look out for" or "Beware of" warning posted before the eyes and ears of the Philippian Christians carries two messages. First, the danger to the church is such as to arouse in Paul the most intense passion. There is no reason to speculate as some do that Paul, in the manner of some

54

preachers, tends to become loudest and most emotional when
treating matters upon which his own convictions are unsettled.
Whether Christians had to obey the law of Moses in order to be
saved was a question fully and finally clear in Paul's mind (Gal.
1:8–9; 2:16). That Paul on occasion spoke positively and ap-
preciatively of his Jewish heritage is true, but that is no proof
that he was ambivalent and indecisive. In many church tradi-
tions, Paul's conversion has been held up as the model for all
conversions; and the model has been drawn, not from Paul (Gal.
1:13–17) himself, but from the vivid and dramatic accounts in
Acts (chaps. 9; 22; 26). When these accounts are embroidered
by the rhetoric of evangelists, listeners are given the impression
that Judaism was for Paul simply a backdrop of black velvet
against which to cast the diamond of his new creation. It is not
difficult to get the further impression that one proof of a genuine conversion is that one speaks of the past only in terms of
regret, rejection, revulsion, and blanket disdain. Paul did not.
Sometimes he visited the quarry from which he was mined and
proudly said, "I myself am an Israelite, a descendant of
Abraham, a member of the tribe of Benjamin" (Rom. 11:1). To
the Israelites belonged the sonship, the glory, the covenants,
the law, the worship, the promises, the patriarchs, and from
them came the Christ (Rom. 9:4–5). For Paul the covenant with
Abraham, who believed God and whose faith was accounted as
righteousness, was still in effect (Rom. 4:1–12). The law of
Moses, given to Israel much later, was good and holy and of
God, serving to teach, restrain, and to make sin clear and evident. Says Paul, though, the law was not intended to be and is
not the means by which one stands acceptable before God.
Justification by law would annul the grace of God and put the
spotlight on human achievement (Gal. 2:16–21). Please understand, says Paul, I am not attacking the Jews. The point is,
salvation does not rest with us but with God. Just as one should
not boast of circumcision, neither should one boast of uncircum-
cision; just as one should not boast of keeping the Sabbath,
neither should one boast of not keeping it. Religious pride is not
the monopoly of the Jews. For Paul it was not the law but the
law moved to the center as the ground of human righteousness
which caused him to yell "Beware!"

55

The second message carried by Paul's threefold warning is
that those preaching the necessity of obeying the law of Moses
were a very real threat to the church. If there was a small Jewish

population in Philippi and hence few church members of that background, that fact alone would not mean the congregation would find little in Judaism to attract them. On the contrary, gentile Christians might be especially enticed by the laws and rituals of a tradition which not only lay behind Christianity but which offered identity, certainty, and promise through its sacred texts. Why would not those gentile Christians find in the Jewish Scriptures, which was after all *their* Bible, commands, practices, and assurances which were most attractive? Not even a Judaizing preacher or teacher would be necessary for questions about obeying the Scriptures to emerge. The history of the church offers evidence enough that issues of continuity and discontinuity are not easily settled. The New Testament itself, especially Matthew, Luke, the epistles of Paul, and Hebrews, struggles with the identity of Christianity in relation to but distinct from Judaism. Marcion's solution was simple: Reject the Old Testament and remove from the New all favorable reference to it. The church, of course, said No, but the presence still of Christian groups such as Seventh Day Adventists and Jehovah's Witnesses testifies to the continuing differences over interpreting the Jewish Scripture in the Christian church.

Who are these who are a threat to the Philippian congregation? Paul's names for them do not help us: dogs (a Jewish term for gentiles; unclean animals; prowlers and scavengers—Paul could have had all or none of this in mind), evil workers, those who mutilate the flesh (3:2). This last phrase translates *katatome*, a parody of *peritome* which means circumcision. In other words, Paul refuses to call them "the circumcision," a term of honor among many Jews, instead calling them mutilators (Gal. 5:12 is similar in mood but more literally means "castrate themselves"). We who accept God's grace in Christ, says Paul, are the true circumcision (3:3; Rom. 2:28). Most likely they are not Jewish Christians, but Jews seeking to win Christians over to the synagogue. Some synagogues were quite evangelistic (Matt. 23:15), but there is no evidence that a synagogue was for Paul an object of attack. However, for some in the church to preach that Christ plus angels equals salvation (Col. 2:8–23) or Christ plus Moses equals salvation (Rom. 10:4–13) or Christ plus circumcision equals salvation (Gal. 2:1–5) or Christ plus anything else, stirred Paul to battle and he never yielded. The issue was the adequacy of the grace of God to make righteous those who trust in that grace.

56

The lines, then, are drawn. Even though Paul was able under other circumstances to say that to Israel belong the covenants, the glory, the sonship, the worship (Rom. 9:1–5), he knows that the intruders in Philippi are preaching a distortion, not just of Christianity but of Judaism as well. Both Paul the Christian and Paul the Jew are violated by these peddlars of circumcision. So he states his thesis: "*We* are the true circumcision, who worship God in spirit, and glory in Christ Jesus, and put no confidence in the flesh" (3:3). "No confidence in the flesh" is the phrase that Paul will now develop. By "flesh" he is referring to the rite of circumcision in particular but in the broader sense "flesh" is a synonym for human effort or achievement (Rom. 10:3).

To develop his thesis Paul draws not upon his library but upon his experience. Were he so minded he could preach the Judaizers' sermon better than they. Paul's claim that he has *more* reason for confidence in the flesh, implies "more than they do." This could mean that while he was born and bred a Jew, the opponents were proselytes, gentile converts to Judaism. If it were the case that they had moved from paganism to Judaism to Christianity, that would help explain their insistence that the Philippians include all the same stops on their religious pilgrimage. It is not a rare occurrence for preachers and teachers to make their own experiences normative for those they seek to lead. If these Judaizers were indeed proselytes and not Jews by birth, their zeal for moving among the churches to complete the faith of the members also becomes more understandable. Although our own experience is no adequate canon for interpreting the text, we cannot avoid the observation that zeal seems to burn more fervently among proselytes than among those "to the faith born." But more importantly for interpreting the text, Paul's list of credentials as a Jew makes more sense if laid beside those of one not born a Jew. For example: circumcised the eighth day (not as an adult), of the people of Israel (not just a Jew religiously), of the tribe of Benjamin (a family genealogy not just a certificate of circumcision), a Hebrew born of Hebrews (probably a reference to his family preserving the native tongue in the home), as to the law a Pharisee (the Jewish party committed to full obedience to the whole law written and oral and not to selected rules such as circumcision), as to zeal a persecutor of the church (the logical conclusion for one tied to the tradition and not as those whose

57

zeal is satisfied with circumcision of Christians), as to righteousness under the law blameless. Can any of the intruders match
such painstaking adherence to the law's demands?

If any of the Philippians were impressed by the Judaizing
preachers, they certainly should now be more impressed by
Paul, even if they had heard this story before (3:1*b*). The sketch
is impressive, especially in the fact that Paul does not extol the
virtues of his new life in Christ by a deprecating description of
his life in Judaism. He does not say of his former life that it was
in the loss column of the ledger, but rather than in his new way
of reckoning he counted gain as loss (v. 7). This difference is
most important. Paul does not say Judaism is worthless, that it
is refuse (garbage, excrement), that intrinsically that way of life
is of no value. What he is describing is his consuming desire to
know Jesus Christ, to be in Jesus Christ, to have that righteousness which is God's gift to the one who believes (vv. 8–9); and
for the surpassing worth of that, he *counts* gain as loss. It is not
the law that is dead; Paul is dead to the law. Paul does not toss
away junk to gain Christ; he tosses away that which was of
tremendous value to him. Therein lies the extraordinary impact
of his testimony and the high commendation of faith in Jesus
Christ. There is absolutely nothing here remotely akin to the
popular type of testimony that catalogs all the sins, frustrations,
empty ambitions, soiled relationships, and foul habits that were
tossed in the garbage can at conversion. Sincere as those may
be, such accounts say in effect that the worth of Christ is greater
than the worst in one's life. What Paul is saying is that Christ
surpasses everything of worth to me. We need to keep in mind
Paul's model in 2:6–11, the Christ who did not relinquish the
low and base for something better, but who gave up all claim
to equality with God in exchange for obedient service. Paul tells
his own story here for the same reason he recited the Christ
hymn: We are not on a path of self improvement, of upward
mobility religiously. If that were the case, then listen to the
Judaizers for there is much gain in what they offer; but if the
"in Christ" mind prevails, then we count opportunities to sur-
pass as nothing. Giving ourselves up to God is total trust, having
no claims, seeking no advantage, but in service to one another
leaving our status before God entirely in God's hands.

58

At the risk of excessive repetition, a summary statement
seems in order here. There are two kinds of religious experience with many adherents which do not have their scriptural

support in Philippians 3:4–9. One is that which finds Christianity a better religion, and therefore attractive to anyone always on the lookout for improvement of one's station, fortune, and peace of mind, not to mention prospects in the hereafter. Paul's testimony as to the "surpassing worth" of life in Christ has to do with abandoning such a search altogether, not having a righteousness of one's own but trusting solely in the grace of God. The other kind of religious experience not supported by this text is that which views the past as totally negative, a failure in every way. Certainly there are those who become Christian out of a background of confused values, wasted opportunities, inner turmoil, and social wreckage. This fact is not to be denied nor treated lightly; but that pattern is not to be imposed upon Philippians 3, as is sometimes done. We do not have in this text the portrait of a man at war with himself, crucified between the sky of God's expectations and the earth of his own paltry performance. Paul is not in this scene a poor soul standing with a grade of ninety-nine before a God who counts one hundred as the lowest passing grade. It is to be regretted that the Revised Standard Version uses "*suffered* the loss of all things" in verse 8 rather than a more straightforward "I treated as loss" or even "I threw away everything." The word "suffered" has opened the door to various psychological analyses more appropriate to Romans 7:15–25 than to Philippians 3:4–16. The Paul of Philippians did not come to faith in Christ out of deep depression because of flaws discovered in himself. On the contrary, as to righteousness under the law, Paul says he was blameless (v. 6).

To counter the Judaizers Paul does not offer the Philippians simply his reasons for moving his membership from the synagogue to the church, but neither does he confine himself to a recitation of the reversal in his life from seeking to claim righteousness to accepting in trust the righteousness God gives in Christ Jesus. He moves on to share with his friends the inner structure of his new life of faith (vv. 10–11). There are no surprises here for there have been glimpses already (1:19–23), but repetition of matters of such importance is not irksome for Paul (3:1). Paul's faith has at its center a desire to know Christ in full identification; to live is Christ, he has said earlier (1:21). This identification means not only relinquishing all claim which would have its counterpart in the Christ's relinquished claim to the divine glory (2:6–7), but also union in the passion of Christ: suffering, death, resurrection (2:8–11). That which needs most

59

to be observed here is the order in which Paul presents the unfolding of Christ's passion in his own life.

Paul ends with resurrection. His reference to resurrection as his final hope (v. 11) is neither unusual nor uncharacteristic. Whether expressed in quiet personal tones or with trumpet blasts, the resurrection from the dead in which Paul hoped to participate was always central in his faith (I Cor. 15:12–58). He has referred to it in Philippians as the day of Christ (1:6, 10; 2:16). The "if possible" (v. 11) is Paul's reminder to himself and to his readers that those who think they stand should take heed lest they fall (I Cor. 10:12). Even one who had preached to others could be disqualified (I Cor. 9:27). The "if possible" may also be a counter to the Judaizers who may have been offering with circumcision guarantees of security before God.

Paul also *begins* with resurrection (v. 10). Again this is not uncharacteristic, for even though Paul always held before himself and his readers the hope of a resurrection like that of Christ (Rom. 6:5, 8; II Cor. 4:14; 5:1–5), he also understood Christ's resurrection as having benefits in the present life of the believer. Because Christ was raised from the dead, a new life is possible for those who die to sin (Rom. 6:2–4). Because Christ was raised and sits at God's right hand, he is interceding in behalf of those who trust in him (Rom. 8:34). Here in Philippians 3:10, Paul speaks of a benefit of Christ's resurrection in terms of power. Although he provides here no particulars as to how that power expressed itself in his life, Paul probably is referring to the enabling of his ministry. Surely that is what the Philippians, who knew so well the terrible adversities under which Paul worked, would have understood by Paul's desire to know the power of Christ's resurrection. Between these references to future and present benefits of Christ's resurrection, however, Paul speaks of sharing Christ's suffering and becoming like him (being con-formed with) in his death (v. 10). We have already had occasion to hear Paul speak of sharing, being partners (the word is often translated "fellowship") in suffering (1:7, 29–30), joining Christ's, his own, and the Philippians' in the closest possible way. Paul understood his ministry not only as preaching Christ crucified but carrying about in his body the death of Jesus (II Cor. 4:10). As Colossians 1:24 expresses it, "and in my flesh I complete what is lacking in Christ's afflictions. . . ." There is no question but that Christ's suffering enabled Paul to interpret his own, and his own suffering enabled him to interpret

60

Christ's. The present point is that although he spoke often of participating in Christ's suffering and death (Gal. 2:20; 6:17), the passage before us is striking in that he places suffering and death *after* resurrection.

In terms of the Christian calendar, Paul put Easter before Good Friday, or to be more precise, in verses 10–11 he speaks of Easter, Good Friday, and Easter. For Paul, the resurrection interpreted the cross, planting it centrally not only in his faith but also in the style of his life and ministry. Rather than erasing Good Friday, Easter was God's vindication of Good Friday as the definition of God's way in the world and for the world: obedience, suffering, death. This is not to say Paul was morbid, meditating on crucifixion scenes, imaging himself hanging on a tree. Taking the form of a servant and being obedient to death took shape in word and deed, in concrete acts of ministry.

Chronologically the calendar is, of course, correct: Good Friday and then Easter; but since the church reads as one of its Lenten epistles Philippians 3:8–14, the text might serve to give the believers a theological calendar: Easter and then Good Friday. This could be especially important in those communities in which Good Friday has been dropped, but Easter services have been multiplied, as though there could be a resurrection when no one is dead. The result for many churches is the loss of both Good Friday and Easter. All that remains is the Saturday between, with the church vaguely sad about the cross and vaguely hopeful about the empty tomb.

In verses 12–14 Paul is again the runner (2:16). The metaphor is familiar but is it a contradiction of his strong declaration only a few verses earlier, that righteousness is by faith and not by works? No, not in Paul's mind. Faith for him involved running, wrestling, striving, and fighting, none of which would end until the day of Christ. We must remember that for Paul all that effort was not for merit but was rather the activity of one who had abandoned all claim to merit. Trust in God's grace did not make Paul less active than the Judaizers but rather set him free now to run without watching his feet, without counting his steps, without competing with other servants of Christ. His goal is clear: to be with Christ in the resurrection. To that end he can seek, because he has been found; he can know because he has been known; he can apprehend because he has been apprehended. In a word, Paul sought to lay hold of him who had already laid hold of Paul. If the Judaizers were offering "Jesus

61

plus Moses equals perfection of faith and total assurance," then the Philippians need to know that Paul is not offering that. The work begun among them will not end until God brings it to completion (perfection) in the day of Christ (1:6). Lest any miss that point, Paul portrays himself in the least relaxed, most demanding posture he knows: as a runner in a race. His language is vivid, tense, repetitious: pressing, stretching, pushing, straining. In those words the lungs burn, the temples pound, the muscles ache, the heart pumps, the perspiration rolls. One's first impression is that Paul may be describing a life so demanding that the Philippians may turn from him to the Judaizers who, even with a gospel of works, offer an easier path; but Paul must be honest. Beyond that, however, he probably knows that smiling presentations of the gospel as the way to be healthy, wealthy, and wise are finally insulting to those who wish to be taken more seriously than that.

What is at stake here is "the prize" (v. 14). It is not fully clear what Paul has in mind when he speaks of "the upward call of God in Christ Jesus." It is not likely that he is referring to his apostolic call, because it must be something as much a goal for the church as for himself. Turning private experiences into public demands is cruel and non-productive. As all Christians are the "called," he probably is speaking of the call to faith in God through Jesus Christ, a call which has its fulfillment in the presence of God. We should hasten to note that call to faith and call to ministry are not separated in Pauline thought. His own account of his call to apostleship includes his "conversion" (Gal. 1:13–17). The records in Acts of his Damascus road experience also interweave the two calls. The church has not departed from this fundamental conviction, that one's baptism is also an ordination to ministry and service.

In pursuit of that prize Paul not only strains forward but he forgets what lies behind. Whether he is speaking of his former life in Judaism with his remarks intended polemically is uncertain. Three phrases in this passage indicate he still has these intruding preachers in mind. One of these is the expression "forgetting what lies behind." The Judaizers were preaching the authority of the ancient Mosaic tradition. The other two are the uses of "perfect" in verses 12 and 15 (the RSV translates it "mature" in v. 15). If, and we only conjecture here, an appeal of the Judaizers was that one became a complete, fulfilled, perfect Christian by obeying the law fully, accepting circumcision

62

as the sign of the people of God, then verses 12 and 15 would address that matter strongly, and sarcastically. According to this reading of the text, Paul would be saying in verse 12, "I had better credentials than any of them, discarded them all, and in no way regard myself as complete or perfect." In verse 15, he would be addressing the church perhaps with some humor: "Since perfect also means mature or grown up, then it is true of some of us—we are perfect." This use of the word in the sense of maturing in faith and love is not uncommon for Paul (I Cor. 2:6—3:3; 13:11). It is regrettable that popular usage of the word "perfect" ("Nobody is perfect") almost always means "flawless in morals," a definition that hardly fits any of the many New Testament uses of the word.

Having said all that, even if Paul at this point no longer has the Judaizers in mind but is rather calling the Christians to continued growth and maturity, the message to the church remains clear. Even if forgetting the past refers not to Judaism but to one's Christian yesterdays, forgetting could still be appropriate. After all, who is keeping score? Even sound advice, though, should not be pushed to absurdity. Neither Paul nor we should erase completely the memory. The central act of worship is an act of memory: "Do this in remembrance." Even the church itself cannot be experienced in its fullest and widest fellowship without memory's aid: "I thank my God in all my remembrance of you" (1:3). Also, of course, progress toward maturity is not served by indiscriminately forgetting the past. Paul knows that; in fact, he says as much in closing his comments begun in 3:1*b*: "Only let us hold true to what we have attained." In other words, let us not abandon the line of march by which we have come this far.

The Philippians were to understand that the line of march or disciplined path (in academic circles Paul's term meant "the fundamentals") was not simply a matter of duplicating Paul's experience. His background was Jewish; theirs most likely was not. Who we *were* affects how we experience Jesus Christ. Paul will not abandon his fundamental principle that while we are one body, not all have the same gifts nor the same functions (Rom. 12:4–8). So when he comes to his principal term for exhorting the Philippians, "be minded" or "have this mind" (v. 15), he modifies slightly his earlier usage. When he offered the Christ model in 2:5–11, he said without qualification, "Have this mind," but now, when offering himself as model, he says, "Be

63

thus minded, and if in anything you are otherwise minded. . . ." God sheds upon the path light that is not mediated through Paul. The whole truth is not pulled through the knothole of one person's experience. God may lead the church around, beside, beyond, or even in spite of its leaders, and a mark of a great leader is to be able to say just that. However, no great leader allows that truth to justify abandoning the church to the confusion of relativism, to be victimized by everyone who comes to town blessing some gross error with a proper text. God may have new and different understandings in store for you, yes; but let us continue to walk, says Paul, within the basic guidelines by which we have progressed thus far (v. 16).

Philippians 3:17—4:1
Look to Paul Rather Than to the Libertines

In this passage Paul draws the lines as sharply as he did in 3:2 and with descriptions of the troublemakers which, as in 3:2, amount to name calling. On the one side are Paul and others like himself who are examples of conduct to be imitated (v. 17). On the other are many who live as enemies of the cross, whose god is the belly, whose glory is their shame, whose minds are on earthly things, and whose end is destruction (vv. 18–19). As for Paul and his associates, their minds are not upon earth but upon heaven from which Christ will come as Savior. One of Christ's saving acts will be the changing of the body, lowly and frail, to the form of Christ's own glorious body (vv. 20–21). Apparently both groups are in the church and understand themselves as offering to the Philippians a Christian lifestyle. Since Paul has told the Philippians of this other group (and they are many, v. 18) on repeated occasions and now again with tears, they clearly are not a danger in the distance. They have had or are now beginning to have enough success in attracting Philippian Christians that the apostle, unable to throw himself between them and the church except by letter, weeps over his own words.

64

Who are these "enemies of the cross"? Paul's description of them does not fit either the opponents of 1:27–30 or the competitive preachers of 1:15–18 whose motives were unworthy but who nevertheless were preaching Christ. Are they, then, the dogs and evil workers of 3:2? A number of commentators think so and take 3:17 as the resumption of the intense emotion with which Paul began his attack. How one identifies the group determines one's understanding of the phrases in verses 18–19. If they are Judaizers, then Paul's terms for them could be quite plausibly interpreted as follows: They are enemies of the cross in that they glory in perfection of faith in obedience to the law rather than embracing the cruciform life; their god is the belly, in that food laws are very important; they "glory in their shame" refers to the exposure of the body in the rite of circumcision; and "minding earthly things" is attending to sabbaths, new moons, regulations as to the clean and unclean. Likewise, with Judaizers in mind, Paul's remark about the lowly body being changed to a glorious one could be taken as the alternative to changing the body by circumcision.

However, it is most likely that 3:17—4:1 addresses a problem different from that represented in 3:1*b*–16. The issue with Judaizers had to do with one's status before God; that is, is righteousness claimed by observance of the law or is it the gift of God to the person of faith? The issue in 3:17–4:1 has to do with conduct and specifically with attitude toward and use of the physical body. By whatever name they should properly be identified, the persons about whom Paul warns the church represent a libertine lifestyle, perhaps even antinomian. Granted the awkwardness for the reader to have Paul shift suddenly from battling on one front to battling on another, that is not a difficulty as great as attributing indulgence of fleshly appetites to the regulation-minded intruders addressed earlier. And Paul's description of the troublemakers in verses 18–20 is clearly that of persons who represent indulgence of the body as an expression of the new life in Christ. They are not theoreticians to be countered with reason and logic; they actually live (walk) in a way that, in Paul's mind, opposes the gospel and the word of the cross. Food and sex are to them god and glory (vv. 19–20). Since the body is the center of this lifestyle, the end of the body is their destruction.

As foreign to Christian behavior as this may seem, it is not difficult to understand how some could arrive at such a view. The missionary preachers had proclaimed freedom in Christ. Paul himself was a foremost preacher of freedom. To Jewish ears that message might come as a call to cast off the yoke of

65

restraint, the burden of all regulations. What more natural way to demonstrate one's freedom than indulgence in the areas of former restriction? To gentile ears that message might come as a call to be rid of the physical hindrances to one's free spirit, one's eternal soul. What more natural way to show that the body, once a prison for the soul, is no longer in control than by treating the body as totally irrelevant to the spiritual life? Total indulgence, like total abstinence, announces that the body is not involved in one's true identity as spirit. Other letters of Paul testify often to this interpretation of Christian freedom by some in the churches. In Galatia (5:13–24), in Rome (6:5–23; 16: 17–18), in Corinth (I Cor. 5:1–11): Wherever Paul's gospel of freedom from law was heard, it was also misheard. Some, perhaps, were too immature to see that liberty-become-license is really a new kind of bondage. There were others, however, who "do not serve our Lord Christ, but their own appetites (bellies), and by fair and flattering words they deceive the hearts of the simple-minded" (Rom. 16:18).

One further word needs to be said about the identity of those about whom Paul warns the church. Some recent scholars have accounted for the presence of both nomian and antinomian elements in Pauline churches not by identifying one as Judaizers and the other as libertines but by understanding both as descriptive of Jewish Christian Gnostics. Gnosticism (literally a gnostic is "one who knows") is a term given by modern scholarship to a view widely held in the world of early Christianity which was at its center dualistic. This is to say, matter and spirit are opposing realities; matter is evil and spirit is good. Human beings are spirits trapped or imprisoned in material bodies and living as lost aliens in a hostile material universe. Salvation comes, however, by the knowledge that we are spirit, from a spirit realm and returning to a spirit realm. To one who has this knowledge, the world, society, the body, all things physical are nothing, to be treated with disregard. Salvation is liberation by *knowledge,* and one way Jesus could be fitted into such a perspective was to regard him as the revealer, the bringer of this knowledge. To be identified as Jewish Christian Gnostics a group would have to interpret Jesus Christ, the gospel, and the life of the believer so as to embrace elements of both Judaism and Gnosticism. Some New Testament scholars such as Walter Schmithals *(Paul and the Gnostics)* are convinced that the troublemakers in Corinth, Galatia, Thes-

66

salonica, and Philippi exhibit exactly those traits.

The jury is still out as to whether this is a proper reading of the evidence. The issue is not whether Jewish and Gnostic elements existed in some churches, even within the same churches. Paul's letters, including Philippians, address such tendencies. The issue is whether they reflect the presence of a single group which we could name Jewish Christian Gnostics. If anyone doubts that views as disparate as those represented by these three terms could possibly exist in a single belief system, then a careful look around at the church will quickly dissolve that doubt. It is not difficult to find in a single congregation or group or, for that matter, a single person, compounds of unbending legalism, strong personal attachment to Jesus Christ, and dualistic spirituality that rejects all involvement in matters economic, political, or social and assumes no responsibility for the human condition. In fact, to be even more confessional, most of us could look within ourselves and find the residue of all these views and more, still lodged confusedly, unreasonably, but no less really in the strange constellations of faith.

Uncertainty as to the full identity of the persons posing a threat to the church at Philippi does not, however, make any less certain the point at which Paul sensed their posing the gravest danger. The characteristic of the opponents of 3:17— 4:1 most offensive to Paul was their conduct, and it is at that point he counters them. Against their lifestyle he offers his own and that of others whose example is to be emulated. The phrase "join in imitating me" (v. 17) perhaps creates discomfort in us not only because of its egotistical ring but also because of the artificiality we associate with imitation. Some of that discomfort may be dispelled by the realization that imitation of the teacher or the master was a pedagogical principle held in high regard and widely practiced. Philosophers, moralists, masters of academies, as well as religious leaders espoused and practiced the principle. It assumed a special kind of relationship between teacher and pupil, master and disciple that is rare today; and it placed a burden upon those who taught and led, which few are willing any longer to accept. The fundamental presupposition of the method, however, remains unquestionably true: The behavior, the lifestyle of a person has a profound impact upon others. Surviving all the bad jokes about piety and the frequent indictments of shallow moralisms is Paul's word for the Christian life: "walk" (translated "live" in vv. 17–18). To show them how to walk, those first generation believers, with no precedents or history, with no New Testament, with few preachers and most of them itinerant, struggling as a small minority in a pagan culture, no better textbook could be offered than the lives of those who stood before them as leaders.

As Paul countered lifestyle with lifestyle, so he countered teaching about the body with teaching about the body. Paul's view of the human body was not formed in reaction to those who indulged their physical appetites. Denial of the body in rites of abstinence can be the reverse side of the same problem of inordinate attention to the flesh. Severity to the body ("Do not handle, Do not taste, Do not touch") is "of no value in checking the indulgence of the flesh" (Col. 2:21–23). This is a truth vital to the church's life, but difficult to learn. It is a rather common notion that the Christian answer to indulgence is abstinence, and the notion finds frequent expression during Lent. Since Philippians 3:17—4:1 is often a Lenten reading, this text could help worshipers experience Lent at a more significant level. After all, the Kingdom of God is neither partaking nor abstaining "but righteousness and peace and joy in the Holy Spirit" (Rom. 14:6–17). As a Jew and as a Christian Paul accepted the body as created of God and as an integral part of one's identity. It is not a substance foreign to our true nature. Naturally enough, then, Paul's doctrine of resurrection was just that, resurrection from the dead and not the survival of an immortal soul free at last. As far as the body was concerned, resurrection meant the transformation of this lowly body to conform to Christ's glorious body (v. 21). What that transformed body would be like Paul sought once to explain (I Cor. 15: 35–50), but not to everyone's satisfaction. The transformation will be the work of Christ, who, by virtue of his lordship at God's right hand, has the power to subject everything in creation to himself (v. 21; cf. also 2:11; I Cor. 15:24–28). "All things" was a technical term for the totality, all that exists; and the last force to be subjected is death.

The triumphant note with which Paul concludes at 3:20–21 is similar and yet dissimilar to other eschatological passages in his letters (I Thess. 4:13–18; I Cor. 15:51–57). That Christ will come from heaven and effect the transformations described is affirmed in all of them. Only in 3:20 does Paul call Christ "Savior," and only in this place does he say our commonwealth (home, citizenship) is in heaven. "Commonwealth" would have

68

been especially meaningful in Philippi with its high patriotism as a Roman colony. We are, says Paul, a colony of heaven (cf. earlier remarks on the same word at 1:27). If anyone is tempted at this point to draw together all of Paul's references to the end time in order to distill from them his doctrine of the eschaton, let the temptation pass. Paul resists all such efforts. He can speak of going to be with Christ and of Christ coming to effect the resurrection; he can describe the time as being as quiet as a last breath and as noisy as trumpeting angels; he can confine the end to a prison cot and he can spread it across the cosmos. In every description, however, that day will be the day of Christ.

In his closing appeal to the church to stand firm against all intruders and disturbers of their common life, Paul repeats his terms of affection for these people. What they mean to him now he expresses with words of love and longing; what they will be to him on the day of Christ he expresses with "joy and crown" (4:1). The phrase depicts the end of a race or contest as a scene of merriment and victory. If the Philippians stand firm, then that will be the scene for Paul on the day of Christ: He will not have run in vain (2:16). Paul used the phrase in writing to one other congregation; interestingly enough, it was to the other Macedonian church in the neighboring city of Thessalonica (I Thess. 2:19–20). The tones of joy and affection in both Philippians and First Thessalonians testify to the profound pleasure these churches provided Paul as a human being, as a Christian, and as a minister.

Philippians 4:2–3
Let Paul's Associates and Fellow-workers Be Reconciled

Paul returns to the problem of dissension which had occupied him earlier (2:1–16), using the very same admonition directed to the congregation (2:2) to address two women who are leaders in the church. We do not know the substance of the quarrel, whether or not it was related to the issues drawing Paul's fire in chapter 3, but we can be sure the dispute was not inconsequential. We know this not because the disputants are

69

leaders (leaders are as capable of pettiness as others) but because the matter draws Paul's attention and he brings it to the attention of the whole church. Paul is not just trying to embarrass two members by having their names read aloud in a worship service. When he dips into an earlier paragraph for two expressions addressed to the whole church, striving or laboring side by side (1:27) and being of the same mind or attitude (2:2), he is reminding them that leaders are not exempt from the standards expected of the membership in general. Beyond that he is reminding them that they are leaders and therefore are able by words or deeds to polarize the congregation, destroying the one soul, one mind, one body. To accept a leadership role is to accept responsibility beyond private preferences. Basic to his admonition is the fact that both these women are friends and associates, fellow workers with Paul. They have been members of that circle Paul calls "side by side athletes"; and if common suffering, common joy, common work, common faith mean anything, then memories of the road traveled together should heal this wound.

Paul mentions these two in a letter to be read to the church because he expects the church to help with the healing. Notice that Paul does not, as some pastors do, regard matters such as this as private, to be settled outside the church lest anyone be disturbed. No, in Paul's view, this is precisely the nature and function of the congregation as a partnership. Being members of one another means laying before each other joys, sorrows, and burdens, but also issues to be settled (I Cor. 6:1–6). Since the whole congregation is to share in such work, there will be, as in the case here, occasions when the membership ministers to its leaders. What a compliment to the maturity of the church that Paul gives them this opportunity; we can hope Euodia and Syntyche were mature enough to accept the church's help.

In several ways we are reminded by this brief paragraph that we are reading someone else's mail. Paul and the Philippians knew the nature of the quarrel; we do not. Paul and the Philippians knew the identity of the one called "true yokefellow"; we do not. It may have been a leader of the church, the whole church addressed as one person, or the word translated "yokefellow," *Synzygos,* may have been a proper name. Paul and the Philippians knew who Clement was; we do not. Attempts to identify him with the late first century elder of the Roman church in whose name we have a letter have not been

70

persuasive. Two things, though, we do know: one, that these and all laborers in the gospel are known to God and their names are in the book of life (Luke 10:20, "heaven"; Rev. 3:5; 13:8; 20:12–15). Two, we know that, for all the dispute about Paul's attitude toward women, they are very visibly and significantly present in his references to associates in ministry. Women preached and prayed in Paul's churches (I Cor. 11:5) and their names are many in Paul's remembrances of a lifetime of shared service (Rom. 16:1–16). In fact, Luke says the church at Philippi was begun when Paul went to a place of prayer and "spoke to the women who had come together" (Acts 16:13).

Philippians 4:4–7
Once More Rejoice

The refrain of joy resumes now that Paul has attended to the distasteful but necessary admonitions. As said earlier, the word *rejoice* can also be translated farewell; context aids the decision in each case. Here the inclination is toward farewell because verses 4–7 have the clear ring of a closing word. In fact, verses 5*b*–7 may not only be a benediction, but may be a benedictory formula which Paul is quoting. Paul quite often inserts benedictions in the body of a letter (Rom. 11:33–36; 15:5, 6, 13, 33) and the sense of verse 4 calls for *rejoice* rather than *farewell*. The New English Bible says both. What Paul urges, apparently, is that the church not be victimized by its problems within and without. The joy and forbearance (gentleness, II Cor. 10:1) which constitute part of the church's witness to the world (vv. 4–5*a*) are genuinely grounded in the church's faith. Two of the tenets of that faith form a parenthesis around them not only making joy and gentleness possible but liberating them from anxiety. On the one side is the affirmation, "The Lord is at hand." Most likely Paul meant this eschatologically, an expectation he never lost (Rom. 13:11; I Cor. 16:22*b*). However, it may also be taken in the sense of the present experience of the church. By using Philippians 4:4–9 as a lectionary reading near the close of the Pentecost season (the Lord has come in the Holy Spirit) and prior to Advent (the Lord will come), the church has appropriated both meanings. On the other side the parenthesis

71

closes with the affirmation "And the peace of God . . . will keep your hearts and your minds in Christ Jesus." The peace which the church can know, the sense that all is well, does not have its source within—there is dissension—nor without—there is opposition—but in God. In a striking paradox, Paul describes this peace with a military term: The peace of God "will stand sentry watch" over your hearts and minds.

Because the day of Christ is near and because the peace of God stands guard, the church can rejoice. In the face of abuse and conflict the Philippians do not have to press their case. They are to stand firm, yes, but they can be forbearing not overbearing. In full confidence of their trust in God, they can devote time to prayer, praise, and thanksgiving. To their petitions Paul does not offer direct, immediate, and recognizable answers. Rather they can offer both thanks and petitions in the assurance of God's care which surrounds them before, during, and after their prayers. Because God's peace is on duty, they do not have to be anxiously scanning the horizon for new threats. Alert, yes; anxious, no. "Have no anxiety about anything" (Matt. 6:25–34.) here applies to nervous, doubt-filled concern for their own well being and is not to be taken as a blanket endorsement of total indifference to the conditions of others. In other words, this is no scriptural warrant for not caring. After all, Paul said his reason for sending Timothy to Philippi was his genuine anxiety for their welfare (2:20). And Paul himself knew "the daily pressure upon me of my anxiety for all the churches" (II Cor. 11:28). Obviously there is appropriate as well as inappropriate anxiety.

Philippians 4:8–9
Practice the Virtues
Paul Himself Has Embraced

For the second time Paul says "Finally" (3:1; 4:8). Whether 4:8 is a return to 3:1 after a digression or is the conclusion of what once was a separate letter, as some scholars believe, this passage is a conclusion and, like 4:4–7, ends with a benediction. It seems as though the apostle realizes that he has spoken so much of opposition and conflict between the culture and the church that points of commendation and agreement have been overlooked. In 4:8–9 he remedies that somewhat by commending to the Philippians a list of admirable traits drawn from Greek moralists: the true, the honorable, the just, the pure, the lovely, the excellent, the praiseworthy. These were the virtues extolled by the ethicists of Greek culture. Use of such lists not only of virtues but also of vices (Rom. 1:20–32; I Cor. 6:9, 10; Gal. 5:19–21) was a common practice for Paul, just as the Jewish community had done for generations (cf. Wisdom of Solomon). It was not as though Paul were looking for a point of accommodation, an opportunity to embrace his culture. Rather Paul faced a phenomenon with which he and all Christians have had to deal: Outside the circles of Jewish and Christian faith are those men and women whose conduct and relationships exhibit qualities enjoined upon those within those circles. How can persons nurtured in philosophies and religions broadly classed as pagan embody virtues appropriate to believers in God and in Jesus Christ? The fact that this was and still is an undeniable fact has been to some Christians a strange embarrassment rather than a condition to be celebrated. The church that takes a rigid over-against-the world posture is now and again forced to go in search of a more adequate theology.

For Paul and many other Christian thinkers, the doctrine that the one God created all things and all persons provided a way, not to close the eyes to evil, but to be open to the ways and works of God whenever and wherever they appear. The redeemer God is also the creator God and Jesus Christ is the one Lord "through whom are all things and through whom we exist" (1 Cor. 8:6). In Paul's view, some of what can be known of God has been revealed through what God has created (Rom. 1:19–20). It is possible then, says Paul, for a person not born to the chosen people to do what the law of Moses commanded (Rom. 2:14–15). That same line of thought would make room for Paul to include in instructions to Christians the loftiest ethical ideals of the philosophers of his age. Such is the text before us and such is the reason it contains words that are not the usual Pauline terms. In fact, some of these words occur nowhere else in all the Pauline epistles.

Paul's repeating of this virtue list is not given to the Philippians for thoughtless embrace. Notice the qualifications. First, Paul says "think about these things" (v. 8). The word here means to consider, give thought to, reason out. This is not his

73

oft-repeated "have this mind," which he uses when relating the Christians to each other and to Christ. Secondly, Paul offers his own life as a screening room; those virtues which you have learned, received, heard, and seen in me, do these. His expression "learned and received" refers to passing along a tradition. There is a body of teaching giving identity and continuity to the Christian community. Finally, Paul brings the list of virtues and compliance with it under the rule and blessing of the God of peace. In the final analysis, the God who "is at work in you, both to will and to work for his good pleasure" (2:15) speaks the concluding word of approval or disapproval over all human behavior.

Paul Is Grateful for the Church's Relationship with Him

PHILIPPIANS 4:10–20

That 4:10–20 is a distinct literary unit and can be treated as such in the teaching and preaching of the church is beyond question. Some lectionaries offer this passage as a Pentecost reading but begin it at verse 12, a decision based on the practical concern for financing the church's mission rather than on the literary signals in the text itself. The joy formula, not uncommon in Hellenistic correspondence as an introduction to the body of a letter, opens the unit (v. 10) and a doxology closes it (v. 20). So clearly do verses 10 and 20 open and close the passage that some have argued for this as a separate letter of thanksgiving. Added to that evidence is the observation that one would hardly expect Paul to treat a matter as important as the gift from Philippi after he had twice said "And finally." However, it has been pointed out that Paul used the introductory joy formula to begin new discussions within the body of letters, Philippians 4:10 and Philemon 7 being two examples (John White, "Introductory Formulae in the Body of the Pauline Letter," pp. 95–96). Neither has it been persuasively shown that the present location in the letter makes Paul's response to the gift seem of minimal importance to him. In fact, even though the case for 4:10–20 as a separate letter has been strongly argued (F. W. Beare especially), there are other considerations within the passage itself which point to its present location as Paul's own decision.

Treating as a postscript his response to the gift brought by Epaphroditus from Philippi (v. 18) seems quite appropriate to the content of the response itself. As literature 4:10–20 is a gem; as a note of thanks to close friends who have sent a gift, the

75

passage is full of surprises. This is true not only when we read it against the background of our own experience of sending and receiving such notes but also when read against the background of the remainder of the letter. Paul and the Philippians do not represent what one would regard as a standard apostle-church relationship. The Philippians were his partners: In the gospel (1:5), in prison and court defense (1:7), in conflict and suffering (1:30), and unlike all the other churches, they shared repeatedly in financial support of his ministry (4:15–16). Paul held them in his heart (1:7), he yearned for them with the affection of Christ (1:8), he loved and longed for these friends who were his joy and crown (4:1). Expressive of their mutual love, the church sends one of their members to Paul with a gift. In his response Paul never uses the word thanks. He chides them a bit with "now at length" ("after so long," NEB) and his immediate modifier, "you had no opportunity" (v. 10), does not fully dull the edge of the reproach. He feels it necessary to say that he did not really need the gift (v. 11) nor did he seek it (v. 17). Paul gives a brief testimony to the effect that he has contentment in either abundance or want and being in Christ is adequate for all situations (vv. 11–13). After commending their kindness in the act which more than once had occurred (vv. 14–16), Paul makes sure they understand that his desire was not for the gift but for the fruit or profit from it (apparently referring to his ministry, 1:22) which would be credited to their account (v. 17). As far as he himself is concerned, he says, "I have received full payment, and more; I am filled . . ." (v. 18). The language here is that which was common to the world of commerce: "I give you my receipt . . . I am paid in full" (NEB). Paul then shifts from commercial terms to the language of liturgy, designating their gift to him as in reality a sacrifice to God who would in return supply all their needs (vv. 18–19). "God be praised forever. Amen." This is his "Thank you" note, and apparently offered as a kind of postscript!

One has to wonder how the church reacted to this response to their gift. Needless to say, commentators have been somewhat puzzled by it. Descriptions of 4:10–20 have included terms such as tense, detached, awkward, distant, and discourteous. The most generous comment spoke of the passage as evidence of Paul's being human. Efforts to explain Paul's writing in this vein have been many and varied. Some have accounted for Paul's detached air by speculating that the Philippians had

76

resented something Paul had said in an earlier note of thanks, a note now lost to us. This, they say, would explain Paul's businesslike, "Here's your receipt—paid in full." Others have remarked upon Paul's stoicism, never allowing his spirit to rise and fall with circumstance. Certainly Paul comes closer to stoicism here than elsewhere in his letters, even using a favorite expression of the Stoics, to be content (v. 11). Still others find here a residue of legalism in Paul and portray the apostle, for all his preaching of grace, still unable to receive a gift. This awkwardness, it is reasoned, accounts for Paul's unusual language in this passage, five of his words appearing nowhere else in his letters or in the entire New Testament. In addition, quite a few writers have tried to justify Paul's lack of intimacy by reminding us of the power of isolation in a prison cell to rob a person of zest, of appetite, of interest in anything. Under such conditions one cannot remain sensitive and vulnerable and still survive. Some hardened indifference cushions against pain, humiliation, and disappointment.

In these comments, discomforting as they may be, lie fragments of truth and partial explanations for these unusual lines from Paul. Perhaps we would be further helped by recalling the overall tenor of the letter. More than once we have been struck by both the intimacy and the distance expressed by Paul, captured in his phrase, "whether or not." Our life of partnership in the gospel, Paul said to them, depends neither upon my being present or absent. The advance of the gospel does not depend upon my being executed or being set free. My relationship to Christ, he said, does not depend upon living or dying because to live is Christ and to die is to be with Christ. His relationship to the Philippians, his return to them, his execution, his witness, their witness: everything has to be set in the context of the gospel and the meaning of life in Christ Jesus.

In the same way their gift must be understood. Perhaps Paul does feel some inner conflict between the need to express pleasure over the gift and at the same time witness to his freedom from the victimizing power of material things. He knew long before Gustave Flaubert said it that "Of all the winds that blow on love, the demand for money is the coldest and most destructive." Perhaps Paul had grown suspicious of the entanglements of gifts; after all, his freedom to preach unhindered was priceless to him. Repeatedly he had refused to accept

77

money from churches even though he had the right to live by the gospel (I Cor. 9:3–18). Now he finds himself in the situation of having received once and again (v. 16) gifts from Philippi. It is therefore important, perhaps even necessary, for Paul to state again his freedom, to relate the gift to ministry (the fruit which increases from it, v. 17) and to God (a fragrant offering to God, v. 18) and not to himself personally. In other words, the intimacy of giving and receiving must be balanced with distance, discourteous as it may sound. So Paul reminds his friends that he is free. He is able to live with abundance, but it is not necessary that he have it. He is able to live in hunger and want, but it is not necessary that he be poor. He is defined neither by wealth nor poverty but by a contentment that transcends both and by a power in Christ which enables him to live in any circumstance. It is important for his friends to see their gift in this context. The man to whom they sent it was not pacing his cell, inquiring of the guard every five minutes whether the mail had come. Their relationship to that man was not based on gifts and it would not be broken by the lack of them. As long as that is understood, said Paul, "I rejoice in the Lord greatly that now at length you have revived your concern for me": "It was kind of you to share my trouble."

We should not leave this passage without commenting upon the unusual number and variety of images and analogies used by Paul. Drawn from many sources, these words and phrases are put in the service of the gospel to inform, clarify, and enrich Paul's communication. We have already noted his use of a key term drawn from the Stoics (v. 11), but Paul also pulls from mystery cults the word translated "I have learned the secret" (v. 12). In the cults the term referred to the rite of initiation into the mysteries. In the New English Bible, it is translated, "I have been thoroughly initiated." Paul's drawing upon two entirely different religious sources in that culture in order to express himself should give caution to efforts to identify his pre-Christian background on the basis of his vocabulary. As to the frequent use of commercial and business terms in verses 15–18 (records, receipts, interest, credit, paid in full, accounts of giving and receiving) to which we have already alluded, one further comment needs to be made. Paul certainly did not suffer from an inability to relate matters spiritual and material. He did not, as is the case with some Christian leaders, talk apologetically about money and the meeting of basic creature

78

needs as though these were necessary evils. On the contrary, he found it most appropriate to urge the Corinthians to give to the poor by reminding them that Christ was rich in glory but became poor for our sake (II Cor. 8:1–9). Notice the mixing of material and spiritual categories of rich and poor. He does the same here in verse 19: God will meet your needs "according to his riches in glory." Or again, Paul told the Christians in Rome that he hoped his trip to Jerusalem with money for the poor, given by the gentile Christians to Jewish Christians, would bring healing to divisions in the body of Christ (Rom. 15:25–31). Money was not only money. Certainly Paul would never say, "We now interrupt our worship to take the collection." Rather the giving and receiving from Philippi prompted Paul to move the whole transaction to the altar. The gifts were "a fragrant offering (Lev. 1:9), a sacrifice acceptable and pleasing to God." Upon reflection, however, readers of Paul realize that not only gifts move him to praise and doxology but every act, every service; in fact, the entire mission of the church and the life of each believer is finally to be understood liturgically. All reconstructions of Pauline theology that omit his prayers, eulogies, benedictions, and doxologies are incomplete and misrepresent the apostle whose talk *to* God was integral to his talk *about* God.

Finally, if less profound certainly no less beautiful, is the metaphor drawn from nature with which Paul opens his response to the gift from Philippi. In verse 10, "you have revived your concern for me" translates an image of spring and the appearance of new growth with blossoms. Paul speaks of the blossoming again of their concern for him. Apparently their partnership with Paul in giving and receiving had experienced a long winter which, Paul hastens to add, was not their fault; it simply was not the proper season. Now it is spring again, their concern has blossomed, and Paul is filled with joy.

79

Further Greetings and Benediction

PHILIPPIANS 4:21–23

In a pattern conventional for correspondence in that culture, Paul brings the letter to a close. The conclusion consists of two parts: a threefold word of greeting: from himself, from his associates, and from the Christians in the city of his imprisonment, and a word of benediction upon the Philippian church.

Paul's first expression of greeting is from himself and is noticeable in two respects. First, it is to each saint (cf. 1:1) as an individualized greeting. Having spoken throughout the letter to "all of you," Paul now wants each member personally to hear a word from him. How was each saint greeted? This leads to the second feature of this first expression of greeting: the word "greet" is in the imperative. Paul does not say "I greet," but calls on someone to greet each person. Whether he is here calling on the reader of the letter or the bishops and deacons (1:1) or each member to take responsibility to greet the others, we do not know. Neither do we know if greeting each other was a portion of the worship service which on this occasion would follow the reading of Paul's letter. If it were, given the contents of the message just received from Paul, the time of greeting would have been especially moving and healing. The second word of greeting is extended in behalf of Paul's associates. We know that Paul had many partners in ministry who were especially helpful during times of the apostle's imprisonment. Through them he was able to continue his work. Of that group, we know the name of only one who was with Paul at this time: Timothy. The third word of greeting is from the Christians in the city of Paul's imprisonment, and especially from one group of them, those of Caesar's household. It is purely romantic to think this refers to members of the royal family. Caesar's household was a term applied to those in Roman civil service, consisting primarily of slaves and freedmen. They numbered in the thousands serving the imperial administration throughout the empire and not in Rome alone. Why greetings especially from these? Perhaps some of them were originally from Philippi; or since Philippi was a Roman colony, perhaps some had formerly served in Philippi and wanted to be remembered. Or it could be that Paul, held in the praetorium (1:13), came most often in contact with Christians in that place. In fact, since "household" was a common designation for units of Christians meeting in a given area (Rom. 16:3–23); apparently there were several household churches in Rome. Compare also I Corinthians 16:19; Philemon 2; I Timothy 3:15; those believers in government service at the scene of Paul's imprisonment may have formed themselves into such a church. Again, we do not know.

Paul's last word is his first word (1:2): "The grace of the Lord Jesus Christ be with your spirit." "With your (plu.) spirit" (sing.) is unusual but may convey no more than Paul's more common "with you." If a special meaning is intended, that meaning lies close at hand in a recurring refrain within the letter itself: " . . . so that whether I come and see you or am absent, I may hear of you that you stand firm in one spirit . . ." (1:27).

BIBLIOGRAPHY

Reading About the Letter of Paul to the Church at Philippi

1. Further reading on introductory matters (authorship, date, literary form)

DUNCAN, G. S. "Letter to the Philippians," *Interpreter's Dictionary of the Bible*, Vol. 3, pp. 787–91. Brief discussions of the major issues of date, place, purpose, and message.

KOESTER, HELMUT. "Letter to the Philippians," *Interpreter's Dictionary of the Bible*, Supplement, pp. 665–66. Most of the article is devoted to the argument for the composite nature of Philippians.

Most of the commentaries listed below discuss the historical and literary questions, especially Beare, Michael, Martin.

2. Further reading on the Christ hymn in Philippians 2:5–11
In addition to the appropriate sections of commentaries:

MARTIN, R. P. *An Early Christian Confession* (London: Tyndale Press, 1960). A published lecture on the form, authorship, and theology of the hymn.

SANDERS, JACK T. *The New Testament Christological Hymns* (Cambridge: The University Press, 1971). Discusses the major scholarly opinions on form, sources, and meaning of this as well as other hymns in the New Testament.

TALBERT, CHARLES H., "The Problem of Pre-existence in Phil. 2:6–11." *Journal of Biblical Literature* 86 (1967), pp. 141–53. Talbert takes the minority view that the hymn does not deal with pre-existence.

3. Further reading on the meaning of the text

LIGHTFOOT, J. B. *Saint Paul's Epistle to the Philippians* (London: The Macmillan Company, 1913 [reprinted: Zondervan, 1953]). This classic is old, has gone through many editions, and remains valuable for word studies in the Greek text.

MARTIN, R. P. *The Epistle of Paul to the Philippians* (Grand Rapids: William B. Eerdmans, 1959). Introduction and commentary along traditional lines, but open, honest, and clear.

MICHAEL, J. H. *The Epistle of Paul to the Philippians* (New York: Harper and Row, 1927). Solid exegesis combined with interesting theories on historical and literary issues.

83

4. Further reading on Paul's thought as context for Philippians

KECK, LEANDER E. *Paul and His Letters* (Philadelphia: Fortress Press, 1979). Carefully combs through Paul's letters to offer the reader Paul the man, Paul the theologian, and Paul the preacher.

SCROGGS, ROBIN. *Paul for a New Day* (Philadelphia: Fortress Press, 1977). Challenges the reader to appropriate in the present Paul's understanding of Christian existence.

5. Literature cited

BARTH, KARL. *The Epistle to the Philippians*. Translated by J. W. Leitch (Atlanta: John Knox Press, 1962).

BEARE, F. W. *The Epistle to the Philippians* (New York: Harper and Bros., 1959).

DEISSMANN, ADOLF. *Paul*. Translated by W. E. Wilson (New York: Harper and Bros., 1927).

DOTY, WILLIAM G. *Letters in Primitive Christianity* (Philadelphia: Fortress Press, 1973).

FUNK, ROBERT W. *Language, Hermeneutic, and Word of God* (New York: Harper and Row, 1966).

-----. "The Apostolic Parousia," in W. R. Farmer, C.F.D. Moule, R. R. Niebuhr, eds., *Christian History and Interpretation* (Cambridge: The University Press, 1967), pp. 248–68.

LOHMEYER, ERNST. *Der Brief an die Philipper* (Meyer Series, 1956[11]).

PALMER, D. W. "To Die Is Gain," *Novum Testamentum* 17 (1975), pp. 203–08.

PLUMMER, ALFRED. *A Commentary on St. Paul's Epistle to the Philippians* (London: Robert Scott, 1919).

POLYCARP, "Epistle to the Philippians," *The Apostolic Fathers*, Vol. I. Translated by K. Lake. LOEB CLASSICAL LIBRARY (Cambridge: Harvard University Press, 1952).

SCHMITHALS, WALTER. *Paul and the Gnostics*. Translated by John Steely (Nashville: Abingdon Press, 1972).

WHITE, JOHN. "Introductory Formulae in the Body of the Pauline Letter," *Journal of Biblical Literature* 90 (1971), pp. 91–97.